BUTCHER

BUTCHER

a play by
NICOLAS BILLON

Coach House Books / Toronto

first edition

For production rights inquiries, contact Pam Winter, Gary Goddard Agency, 149 Church Street, 2nd Floor, Toronto, ON, M5B 1Y4, Canada, 416-928-0299, www.garygoddardagency.com.

Published with the generous assistance of the Canada Council for the Arts and the Ontario Arts Council. Coach House Books also acknowledges the support of the Government of Canada through the Canada Book Fund and the Government of Ontario through the Ontario Book Publishing Tax Credit.

LIBRARY AND ARCHIVES CANADA CATALOGUING IN PUBLICATION

Billon, Nicolas, author
    Butcher / Nicolas Billon.

A play.
Issued in print and electronic formats.
ISBN 978-1-55245-300-1

    I. Title.

PS8603.I44b88 2014   C812'.6   C2014-904405-4

Also available as an ebook: ISBN 978 1 77056 397 1.

To my father, Pierre.

FOREWORD
by Louise Arbour

Harm, hurt, hate, guilt, punishment, shame, pardon, redemption and justice are all intertwined in a reality where the line between offender and victim is often blurred. The greatest harm inflicted on a victim is when, infected with hate, she morphs into the mirror image of her abuser. This is how the cycle of violence is perpetuated, often with increased cruelty and madness.

Fifty years after Nuremberg, international criminal justice was resurrected in an effort to break this cycle of violence and, in the words of the chief Nuremberg prosecutor, to 'stay the hand of vengeance.' Whether this civilizing project will succeed remains to be seen. In the meantime, we struggle with two larger questions: Where can victims find peace if justice is elusive? Can offenders find closure if punishment is not extended to them?

Real peace and closure, it is often said, can only come from forgiveness. Whether forgiveness arises from an inner generosity or merely from an impetus to overcome residual pain and despair, it is a difficult and necessary process for both the offender and the victim. Yet how can the victim forgive her torturer without betraying who she was before the humiliating pain inflicted upon her? In addition, the victim's pain and shame is often aggravated by a sense of guilt for having put herself in that situation. As she prepares to forgive the offender, she may also have to forgive herself, an even more painful process.

In turn, for the perpetrator of heinous crimes – the torturer, the rapist, the cold-blooded killer – justice allows for closure, for a claim that harm has been remedied, that reparation has been made, that the past is now buried. But without a judicial process, the offender is left to deal with his deed by himself, to take ownership of his crimes and, if he is ever to expect forgiveness from his victim, to eventually forgive himself. It is, I believe, a near-impossible task.

This is why the offender becomes a victim of his own crimes, locked forever in the windowless room of his shameful past, destined to remain his ugly self, and delusional about who he is and what he's done.

And this is how justice brings closure and peace. It tells the painful truth and, even in the face of irreparable harm, it helps both victim and offender to forgive each other and maybe, one day, to forgive themselves.

LOUISE ARBOUR *is a former Supreme Court of Canada justice and former Chief Prosecutor of the International Criminal Tribunals for the former Yugoslavia and Rwanda.*

PRODUCTION HISTORY

Butcher had its world premiere on October 17, 2014, at Alberta Theatre Projects in Calgary, as part of the Enbridge playRites Series of New Canadian Plays. The cast and crew were as follows.

Josef Džibrilovo / John Koensgen
Hamilton Barnes / Andrew Musselman
Inspector Lamb / Eric Nyland
Elena / Michelle Monteith
Young Girl / Natalie Julia Marshall

Director / Weyni Mengesha
Production Dramaturg / Laurel Green
Set and Lighting Designer / David Fraser
Costume Designer / April Viczko
Sound Designer / Peter Moller
Composer and Cellist / Morag Northey
Fight Director / Karl Sine
Stage Manager / Johanne Deleeuw
Assistant Stage Manager / Heather Rycraft
Child Supervisor / Jessica Del Fiero

DRAMATIS PERSONAE

Josef Džibrilovo, 75
Hamilton Barnes, 36
Inspector Lamb, 45
Elena, 34
The Young Girl, 12

TIME AND PLACE

The action takes place in a Toronto police station during the early morning hours of December 25th.

STAGE DIRECTIONS

A slash (/) indicates where the next speaker interrupts the current one.

A star (*) before two character names indicates dialogue spoken at the same time.

A NOTE ON THE LAVINIAN LANGUAGE

Christina E. Kramer and Dragana Obradović have created an imaginary South Slavic language, which we've baptized Lavinian. The idea was to create a language that sounds South Slavic but is not identifiable with any single group nor comprehensible to anyone outside the world of the play.

It is a phonetic language, which makes it easier to speak and memorize. Pronunciation keys for all Lavinian dialogue is provided in an appendix, which begins on p. 82.

Since most of the Lavinian is understood within the context of the dialogue, the English translation is provided separately in the appendix. This placement allows for the reading experience to be closer to that of seeing the play performed.

Under no circumstance should the Lavinian be translated in performance (e.g., surtitles).

Josef Džibrilovo: YO-sef Dzhi-BRI-lo-vo

Marko: MAR-ko

Gnivomir Ilić: GNI-vo-mir I-lich

Juraj Plamen: YU-ray PLA-men (NB: *ray* rhymes with *sky*)

Kazimir Mstijov: KA-zi-mir MSTI-yov

Istvak Pasić: IST-vak PA-sich

Danijel: DA-ni-yel

PROLOGUE

Darkness.

The deep, booming sound of something massive crumbling to the ground. A derelict building? The twin towers? Civilization?

A note, human in tone but not in quality, echoes in the dark. It is soon followed by a second dissonant note, then a third ...

The Furies are waking.

There's another soundscape in our world: the relentless pitter-patter of rain. It will echo throughout the space for the duration of our story, and will vary in intensity from soft to violent to diluvial.

SCENE 1

Lights up.

The spartan office of a police station. It is void of personality: greyish walls, metal furniture, industrial lighting.

Those who enter this room often feel queasy: it's the faint wave of institutional nausea.

A small, grilled window provides the only hint of a world beyond. Below the window is a steam radiator. It clangs every now and then.

On top of a filing cabinet is a small, sad-looking Christmas tree with multi-coloured lights.

Slumped on a chair is JOSEF, *dressed in a military uniform that has seen better days. He's exhausted, in part from fatigue but also from years of running and hiding and secrecy. There's a Santa hat on his head.*

Two men loom over him: LAMB *and* HAMILTON.

Lamb wears a cheap but functional suit. He's made a minimal effort to clean up for work.

Hamilton wears a dripping wet trench coat. There's the faint trace of a British accent when he speaks.

Josef is in a daze. A grimace of pain crosses his face. We'll soon find out why.

Hamilton looks at Josef, examines his features. Lamb watches Hamilton.

HAMILTON: Sorry.

LAMB: No?

HAMILTON: No.

LAMB: You're sure?

HAMILTON: I'm sure.

LAMB: Take another look.

Hamilton looks at Josef again.

HAMILTON: I wish I could help, but ... I've never seen this man before.

LAMB: So he doesn't look familiar at all ... ?

Hamilton shakes his head, shrugs.

LAMB: Damn. (*sighs*) I took this shift 'cause I figured it'd be quiet, ya know? But instead, I'm stuck with ... (*half-hearted salute*) Sergeant Santa.

HAMILTON: Has he said anything?

LAMB: Nothing except for ... (*checks his notes*) 'Ne-chu-vi-nicho-rachi.' At least that's what it sounds like. He said it / every time –

JOSEF: (*slurs*) Ne ću vi ničo rači ...

LAMB: Right. That.

HAMILTON: Is he drunk?

LAMB: There's no alcohol on his breath. He was a bit wobbly on his feet, though. He's under the influence of *something*.

HAMILTON: Drugs?

Lamb shrugs.

HAMILTON: And he said that every time you what?

LAMB: Said what?

HAMILTON: The, thing, sentence ... 'Ne-chu-vi'-whatever.

LAMB: Oh yeah. Every time I asked him a question. Why? Any idea what he might be saying?

Hamilton shakes his head.

LAMB: I thought it was Russian at first, but no, it's some obscure Eastern European ... (*checks his notes*) Lavinian.

HAMILTON: I have a colleague who's from there.

LAMB: You think he's up right now?

HAMILTON: Uh ... Not at three in the morning, no.

LAMB: Yeah. It's just ... I called for a translator, but on Christmas Eve? God knows when he'll get here. *If.*
    Oh, and I guess it's technically Christmas now. Merry Christmas.

HAMILTON: ... Thanks.

LAMB: (*indicates his notes*) Anyway, I tried Google translating this but apparently I can't spell for shit because it tells me he's saying, 'I want very much to woo you.'

HAMILTON: I doubt that, somehow.

LAMB: Yeah, otherwise he ain't gonna like my answer. (*glances at Hamilton*) Not that gay isn't, you know ... (*gives a thumbs up*)
    So whaddya make of the whole military uniform? That's / really throwing me off –

HAMILTON: You said he had my card on him?

LAMB: Oh yeah. Wait'll you see this.

Lamb opens a desk drawer and pulls out a metal hook attached to a string. Baited on the hook is a card.

HAMILTON: Jesus.

LAMB: Had this around his neck. Ever seen one before?

HAMILTON: Is that for shark fishing?

LAMB: It's a butcher's hook, you know, for meat. My uncle brought one home for Halloween one year 'cause I was dressing up as Captain Hook. (*holds up the hook and sneers like a pirate*) Yar!

Startled, Hamilton takes a step back.

LAMB: Didn't mean to ... Sorry.

Hamilton gestures, as if to say, 'It's fine.'

LAMB: Anyway. My mom didn't let me use it, she was afraid I'd take some kid's eye out with it ...

Lamb removes the card from the hook and hands it to Hamilton.

HAMILTON: (*reads from the card*) 'Prohapsi me.'

LAMB: Google says it means 'Arrest me' in Lavinian. That's how I figured where he's from. At least I know I spelled it right.

Hamilton flips the card over.

LAMB: That's your business card, yeah?

HAMILTON: ... It is.

LAMB: You see why I'm confused that you don't know him.

HAMILTON: I'm as confused as you are.

LAMB: I'm getting that vibe.

HAMILTON: (*to Josef*) Sir? Sir. (*points to business card*) How did you get my card?

JOSEF: Ne ću vi ničo rači.

LAMB: At least he's consistent.

HAMILTON: (*to Josef*) Did someone give this to you?

LAMB: I don't think he speaks English.

HAMILTON: Yeah. (*looks at Josef*) Does he even understand where he is?

LAMB: Dunno. When the two kids brought him in, he / was a bit –

HAMILTON: Kids?

LAMB: Right, so, these two kids – well, these two young guys or whatever, they show up at the station around midnight or so carrying our friend here. Officer Taylor, the desk clerk – you met him downstairs, on your way in – says, 'Can I help you,' blah-blah-blah, but they just dump Sergeant Santa on a chair and take off.
   (*takes business card from Hamilton*) Is it possible someone's playing a prank on you?

HAMILTON: If so, it's not funny.

LAMB: Yeah, well ... Stranger things have happened. Few months ago we had a teenager drop off his Alzheimer's grandma 'cause he had a date and didn't want to babysit her. (*shakes his head*) Who treats family like that, am I right?

HAMILTON: Yeah.

LAMB: Anyway, it's just the details here that don't make sense, ya know? The uniform? (*picks up the hook*) You can't get this at a hardware store.
   And your business card. (*beat*) Maybe someone thought he'd need a lawyer.

HAMILTON: An intellectual property lawyer?

17

LAMB: Maybe he's a serial downloader.

Hamilton scowls.

Lamb chuckles and puts the hook back in the desk drawer.

LAMB: Is this your first time in a police station or something?

HAMILTON: It is, as a matter of fact.

LAMB: Well, so you know, you're allowed to make jokes in here.

HAMILTON: It's the middle of the night, Inspector.

LAMB: And I woke you up. My bad.
    What I'm trying to figure out is, why use your business card? If I want to leave someone a note, I'll use a Post-it.

HAMILTON: Could he be homeless? Mentally ill? Maybe I gave him money, I don't know, and that's how he got my card ... ?

LAMB: 'Here y'are, my good man, go get yourself a sandwich and oh, here's my card in case you're ever arrested for, you know, *plagiarism* ... '

HAMILTON: Yeah, okay.

LAMB: In any case, I don't think he's homeless.

Hamilton looks at Lamb.

LAMB: The homeless have an unmistakable ... (*taps his finger on his nose*) aroma. He doesn't. And there's no way to say if he's ... (*makes 'crazy' gesture*) I called the CAMHs and psych wards in the area. No one's gone missing.

HAMILTON: It's pretty clear he's drugged, though.

LAMB: Yeah. (*snaps his fingers*) Maybe he was playing hard to get, so the two kids gave him a roofie ...

Hamilton stares at Lamb.

LAMB: I know, I know. My wife says I've got the worst combination ever: a foul sense of humour and lousy timing.

HAMILTON: It's fine. (*beat*) The download joke was okay.

LAMB: Yeah? With two daughters of Internet age, you learn a thing or two about copyright.

HAMILTON: (*smiles, angles to leave*) Anyway –

LAMB: Okay, can I be that guy?

HAMILTON: What guy?

Lamb takes out his phone.

LAMB: The guy who brings up his kids and then immediately shows you their picture?

HAMILTON: ... Sure.

LAMB: I used to hate people who did this. Before I had kids, right? And then I had my own ... (*smirks*) Now I'm that douchebag.

Lamb hands the phone to Hamilton.

LAMB: That's Erin, she's thirteen, and that's Iris, seven.

HAMILTON: They're lovely.

LAMB: Yeah. They're pretty special.
    I finish my shift just in time for presents in the morning.

Hamilton hands the phone back to Lamb.

LAMB: Any kids?

HAMILTON: No.

LAMB: Lucky you, in a way. Because a wife and two daughters? That's a lot of estrogen in the house. I mean, lots of pink, lots of pastel-coloured everything, eh? Yeah. Wow.

But you know what the worst is? The bathroom. Hands down.

So much (*pronounces 'shea' as 'shee'*) shea butter this, pomegranate that ... It's a goddamn fruit garden is what it is. I swear, you could fart in there all day and no one would ever know. (*laughs*)

All right, all right, you know you've hit bottom when the fart jokes start, am I right? (*beat*) Hit *bottom*?

HAMILTON: Oh, yes. I see.

LAMB: Wait, I'll say it for you: 'Shut the hell up, Inspector.' (*laughs*) Oh, I should follow my own advice sometimes.

HAMILTON: (*thin smile*) Don't worry about it. (*puts out his hand*) I'm sorry I couldn't be of more help, Inspector.

They shake hands. Hamilton turns to leave –

LAMB: Look, do me a favour. Stick around for a bit. Just in case we get lucky and the translator shows up.

HAMILTON: Is it ... ? I have breakfast at my cousin's in Brampton / tomorrow, I could use –

LAMB: Of course, I totally understand. But I'm sure you want to clarify the whole business card thing as much as I do, no? Just give me another twenty minutes.

I'll get you a coffee, and I solemnly swear to not make any more jokes. That's a better deal than my wife gets.

Hamilton shrugs and takes off his coat.

LAMB: Thank you. I appreciate it. I'm gonna YouTube some hockey fights to pass the time, if you're interested.

Lamb goes to his desk and takes his empty coffee mug.

Hamilton shakes his coat and hangs it on the back of a chair.

LAMB: Still raining, eh?

HAMILTON: Yeah.

LAMB: Do you remember when we had, you know, *snow* at this time of the year?

HAMILTON: I grew up in England.

LAMB: Doesn't it snow there?

HAMILTON: Occasionally. Lots of rain.

LAMB: Then you must be feelin' right at home, friend. How do you take your coffee?

HAMILTON: Black, thank you.

LAMB: No.
    Trust me. Not black.

HAMILTON: ... One sugar?

Lamb indicates more.

HAMILTON: Two ...

Lamb indicates more.

HAMILTON: Three ... ?

LAMB: It's for your own good.

Lamb goes to Josef.

LAMB: Coffee? (*mimes drinking with his mug*) Do. You. Want. A. Coffee?

Josef nods. Lamb pats him on the shoulder.

LAMB: (*to Hamilton*) Poor guy. Hell of a way to spend Christmas.

Lamb exits and shuts the door behind him.
Hamilton sits and takes out his phone.
Josef watches Hamilton.

JOSEF: (*whispers*) Marko?

21

Hamilton doesn't react.

JOSEF: Marko.

Hamilton looks up from his phone.

HAMILTON: I'm sorry ... ?

JOSEF: Šta laviš vodje?

HAMILTON: I'm sorry. I don't speak Lavinian.

JOSEF: Da, ritsaš. (*beat*) Marko!

HAMILTON: My name is Hamilton Barnes, sir.

JOSEF: Mene ne me preznameš, nelda?

HAMILTON: I'm sorry ... Do you know where you are? (*points to the floor*) A police station. Toronto?

JOSEF: Mi sne vu Torontu!?

HAMILTON: Yes. Toronto.
You didn't know that?

JOSEF: Kato su me nošli? Bio som abrešan ... i nad som vu Torontu ...

HAMILTON: Yes. (*mimes a rectangle*) How did you get my business card?

JOSEF: (*takes his head in his hands*) Isuse, ne nagu dumliti ... Vu rašiju moter, ka su mi doli ... ?

HAMILTON: Are you all right?

Josef looks back at Hamilton.

JOSEF: Marko ... ?

HAMILTON: No no. (*puts hands on his chest*) Hamilton. I'm not who you think I am.

JOSEF: Moe glasči me ne jervoraju ... (*stands up*) Marko –

22

Josef puts weight on his foot and a sharp pain forces him to sit down again.

Hamilton stands up. Josef leans over and unlaces one of his boots, then attempts to remove the boot. He's too feeble.

Josef beckons Hamilton for help.

JOSEF: Ma daj mi pomači stekuti čizle …

Hamilton hesitates, takes a few steps in Josef's direction —

The door handle jiggles.

Hamilton goes to the door and opens it.

LAMB: Thanks, it's not easy with … (*raises the mug and two styrofoam cups in his hands, puts down the coffees*) I bet you couldn't get him to shut up, eh?

Hamilton notices that Josef has stopped fussing with his boot and pretends like nothing happened.

HAMILTON: Actually …

LAMB: He said something?

HAMILTON: Yeah, a few things but I / didn't understand —

LAMB: The whole 'ne-chu-vi' business?

HAMILTON: No. Other things.

LAMB: Huh. Strange that to you, he would … you know. *Talk.*

HAMILTON: Yeah. (*beat*) Well, maybe not, actually.

Lamb raises an eyebrow, as if to say, 'Do tell.'

HAMILTON: I'm pretty sure Lavinia was under Communist rule. He's definitely old enough to have lived through it.

Lamb shrugs.

HAMILTON: The police weren't exactly, you know, guardians of the peace. A lot of people there still have trouble trusting *any* police for that very reason.

LAMB: He doesn't know you're not a cop.

HAMILTON: I don't exactly give off a 'law and order' vibe.

LAMB: (*smirks*) Nope.

Lamb takes the two styrofoam cups and hands one to Hamilton.

LAMB: Well, if he's spooked by cops, he picked the right night: it's a damn ghost ship around here.

Lamb hands the other coffee to Josef.

JOSEF: Vola.

LAMB: What?

JOSEF: (*hand over his heart*) Vola.

HAMILTON: Is he saying 'thank you'?

LAMB: Maybe. (*repeats the gesture to Josef*) Vola?

JOSEF: (*hand over his heart*) Vola.

LAMB: I guess this qualifies as progress.

JOSEF: Vola.

LAMB: Yeah, okay, now wait 'til you try the coffee.
(*to Hamilton*) Hey, so how come you know so much about Lavinia?

HAMILTON: My colleague. Whenever we complain about things here, he goes off about 'back in my day.'

LAMB: That must get annoying.

Hamilton nods.

LAMB: (*sips his coffee*) Holy fuck this is bad. (*points to Hamilton*) Don't drink it before I make you sign a waiver.

Hamilton chuckles and sips his coffee.

HAMILTON: That is ... unspeakable.

Lamb goes to Hamilton and takes his coffee.

LAMB: And I put *four* sugars.

The two men chuckle. Lamb turns to take Josef's coffee –
Josef sips his coffee, nods, and continues to drink it.

LAMB: Communism must've been worse than I thought.

Lamb throws Hamilton's coffee in the garbage.

LAMB: You a hockey fan?

HAMILTON: Not really.

LAMB: Oh no, of course, it's ... soccer, right? No. 'Football.'

HAMILTON: My parents were from Birmingham, so I was a de facto Villa fan.

LAMB: 'De facto' ... You always talk Greek and stuff?

HAMILTON: It's Latin, actually.

LAMB: (*smacks his forehead*) Latin. Right. *Duh.*

HAMILTON: Oh God, I didn't mean –

LAMB: Just pullin' yer leg.
  Explain something to me. I'm asking because I really just don't get it. How do you get excited about a sport where you're lucky if they score *one* goal in a game? That seems crazy.

HAMILTON: Doesn't that happen in hockey?

LAMB: Sure, every now and then. But it's the / exception, not the rule.

Lamb's cellphone rings. He takes it out and looks at the screen.

LAMB: Shit. DW. 'Da Wife.' (*answers phone*) Hey Honey – (*frowns*) Pumpkin, what are you doing up? (...) Well Santa won't come 'til you're asleep. (...) No no, that's one of his rules: he doesn't deliver presents to children who stay up waiting for him. (...) Of course I'm sure, sweetie. You can ask Mommy. (*turns to Hamilton, whispers*) She likes to double-check her facts, the little monster. (...) See? Now that you know, go to bed.

(*turns to Hamilton and makes a 'talk talk talk' gesture*) Honey, I'm *sure* that Santa didn't forget about you. (...) Because he told me. (...) That's right, in fact, he's with me now. He just told me what he's bringing you. (*makes an 'okay' sign to Hamilton*) What? (...) No, I don't think Santa has time to talk to you right now – (...) Of course he likes you, he's just very busy – (...) All right, all right, I'll ask him. (*presses mute button*) Okay, so bad move, telling her I was with Santa. Shit.

(*looks at Hamilton*) Could you be Santa?

HAMILTON: Sorry?

LAMB: Just say hi or whatever, tell her you're in a hurry ... I'd do a voice but she recognizes me now.

HAMILTON: Uh ...

LAMB: Please. She thinks Santa forgot about her.

HAMILTON: ... I guess.

LAMB: Bless your cotton socks. It's Iris, the seven-year-old.
(*presses mute button again*) Pumpkin? Santa's gonna say hello, but he's in a hurry, okay?

Lamb passes the phone to Hamilton.

HAMILTON: Hello?

Lamb places his hands under his diaphragm, miming 'Deep voice.'

HAMILTON: (*deep voice*) Nice to meet you, Iris. (...) Yes, of course this is Santa.

Lamb mouths 'Ho ho ho!'

HAMILTON: (...) Now don't you worry – ho ho ho! – I haven't forgotten about you. You're next on my list ...

Lamb mimes 'Sleep.'

HAMILTON: ... So long as you're asleep, of course. Will you go straight to bed now? (...) That's a good girl.

Lamb gives Hamilton a thumbs-up.

HAMILTON: (...) Good night, Iris. Ho ho ho!

Hamilton hands the phone back to Lamb.

LAMB: Pumpkin? Go to bed now. (...) Yes, Santa's from England. Put Mommy back on the phone. (...) Hey. If she's not asleep in twenty minutes, you have my permission to grind all my Ativan into a glass of warm milk. (...) See you soon, Honey. (*hangs up*)
(*to Hamilton*) Thank you.

HAMILTON: Don't mention it.

LAMB: That was a pretty good Santa.

HAMILTON: Oh, thanks.

LAMB: By the way, I was kidding about the Ativan.

Hamilton shrugs, as if to say, 'Obviously.'

LAMB: Iris, you know, she's starting to have doubts about Santa. Her sister knows he's not real, of course, so I'm sure that isn't helping. But I guess we don't want her to grow up too fast, you know? Let her stay a kid for another year ...

(*sighs*) I gotta tell you, when Carol was pregnant with Iris? I was hoping for a boy. I don't know if that's sexist or whatever, but I guess since we already had Erin and ... I just feel like boys are less naive than girls, maybe? (*beat*) But you know what the toughest thing is?

Hamilton shakes his head.

LAMB: Maybe it's because I'm a cop, you know? I get that. But I'm terrified they're gonna get raped. Keeps me up at night. Erin, she's thirteen, right? She's just starting to have (*mimes breasts, awkward*) ... and every now and then I catch some dude, some guy in his thirties or *forties*, giving her a look and I'm telling you, I wanna go over and fucking break every bone in his body, right? And I know that's wrong, but still, it's *there*, that impulse, you know ... (*beat*) Guys who fuck with children? I'm sorry, but they should get the death penalty. I know that's not politically correct or whatever these days, but seriously ...

(*looks at Hamilton*) Maybe you gotta have kids to understand this, I don't know.

HAMILTON: I don't think so. You want to protect what you love.

Lamb points to Hamilton, as if to say, 'You got it.'

LAMB: But I bet you don't believe in the death penalty.

Hamilton shakes his head.

LAMB: Yeah, no surprise.

HAMILTON: Why do you say that?

LAMB: Well, 'cause, you know ... (*gestures at Hamilton*) Just the way you're ... dressed. Whatever. 'Cause you're educated, I don't know. The accent. You can tell.

HAMILTON: Oh-kay ...

LAMB: No, it's like ... Look, you're the kind of guy who uses words that makes guys like me want to, you know, punch you in the face, that's all. (*quick*) Not literally, obviously. Sorry, that was ... (*sighs*) You like football and, I don't know, *polo* or whatever. I'm a hockey and UFC guy. It's totally cool. (*beat*) Please tell me you've heard of UFC.

HAMILTON: (*nods*) It's cage fighting.

LAMB: You've never watched it.

HAMILTON: Guilty.

LAMB: Course not. No one who did would call it 'cage fighting.' I'll tell you this, friend: it's the sport of the future. It's like boxing meets martial arts. These guys are *warriors*. And there's a whole 'code,' you know? Honour. It's amazing to watch. After these guys finish kicking and punching and kung-fuing the shit out of each other, they hug it out.

HAMILTON: Sounds like bread and circuses, no?

LAMB: Whoa, they're not *clowns*.

HAMILTON: Of course, I only meant ...

LAMB: What?

HAMILTON: Watching people hurt each other just isn't my idea of a good time.

LAMB: They're not people, they're athletes!
     You sound like Carol. She's watched it once or twice and hates it. Says they all look like convicts. With the tats and stuff?

HAMILTON: Right.

Suddenly, Josef coughs violently and puts his head between his legs.

LAMB: Aw shit.

Lamb goes to Josef.

LAMB: What's wrong, buddy?

JOSEF: Pomači mi da odiđem vodavde.

HAMILTON: I think he's feeling sick or something.

LAMB: Thanks, Captain Obvious. (*to Josef*) Okay there?

JOSEF: Rači njimu da bertam vu bolnaku.

LAMB: Right.

Lamb helps Josef back into an upright position.

Josef nods that he's okay, then turns to Lamb and mimes drinking.

JOSEF: Predaj varu, mila makico. Varu?

LAMB: I don't think any more coffee's a good idea.

HAMILTON: Maybe he wants water.

LAMB: Oh yeah. That makes more sense.

Lamb goes out to get water. When the door closes, Josef grabs Hamilton's arm.

JOSEF: Pomači mi da odiđem vodavde!

Hamilton pulls his arm free.

HAMILTON: What the hell is wrong with you?

JOSEF: Ne znomam šta se dečova, okay? Mustam biti nevodje –

HAMILTON: I don't know *who* you think I am, and I have no idea who you are, okay? Do you get it?

JOSEF: Tanko moštrije od žuta dajinog rani, tanda nezahvolno jemamo dejče.

HAMILTON: I don't speak Lavinian!

JOSEF: Ja som ti tažio jidžek, Marko.

Hamilton glares at Josef.

HAMILTON: If – *if* – you are who you say you are, you'd be dead.

JOSEF: Vravaj mi, ne razmozgijem ničo malje nago ti ... Ali ja som, Marko. Tati je.

Hamilton removes the Santa hat from Josef's head.

JOSEF: Da.

The door opens and Lamb returns with a bottle of water. Hamilton steps away from Josef.

LAMB: Here you go, buddy.

Lamb hands Josef the water bottle.

JOSEF: Vola.

Josef drinks. Lamb notices the Santa hat in Hamilton's hand.

HAMILTON: I took it off. It was undignified.

Lamb gives Hamilton a look.
Josef groans and holds his side.

LAMB: (*to Josef*) You better? Okay?

HAMILTON: Should he see a doctor, maybe?

LAMB: Well, as I said, I'm just waiting for the translator.

HAMILTON: He looks like he's in pain.

JOSEF: Bolnaka, bolnaka!

LAMB: Okay, bolnaka, bolnaka! What is it?

JOSEF: (*makes a siren sound*) Bolnaka!

HAMILTON: An ambulance?

LAMB: Jesus.

Josef moans.

HAMILTON: The East General is five minutes away.

LAMB: I can give him some aspirin. But I can't just let him go.

HAMILTON: Inspector, look at him!

LAMB: I get it, I get it ... Give me a second, there's protocol that needs to be followed ...

HAMILTON: Is he under arrest?

LAMB: Well, no, I mean unless he's turning himself in ...

HAMILTON: Why would you think that?

LAMB: Because he had a note that said 'Arrest me.' Written on your business card.

HAMILTON: Right. Though that could've been the two men who ... (*beat*) I just hope his *habeas corpus* rights / haven't been infringed.

LAMB: *Habeas corpus?*

HAMILTON: 'To hold / the body.'

LAMB: Yeah, I know what it *means*, Mr. Barnes. I just feel like all of sudden you're lawyering up. I'm a simple guy, and I may not know the difference between Greek and Latin, but I'm not an idiot.

HAMILTON: I never implied –

LAMB: Nor, for the record, am I a sadist. I can see that our friend here is in pain.

HAMILTON: Of course. I'm sorry if it sounded ... I just don't like to see people suffering.

LAMB: A compassionate lawyer. It must be Christmas. (*beat*) But let me ask you a question. Why's his boot untied?

Hamilton looks at Josef's boot.

HAMILTON: I hadn't noticed.

LAMB: Well, he only could've done it when I went out.

HAMILTON: Yeah.

LAMB: You didn't notice him. Lean over. Untie his boot.

HAMILTON: I was on my phone. (*embarrassed*) Angry Birds.

LAMB: Mr. Barnes –

Suddenly, Josef stands up and heads for the door.

JOSEF: Hodem vu bolnaku.

LAMB: Whoa, buddy!

Josef takes only a few steps before a sharp pain from his foot stops him cold. He grunts and braces himself against the desk.

Lamb and Hamilton carry him back to his seat. Frustrated, Josef brushes them off and starts to unlace his boot again. He indicates he needs help.

LAMB: You want the boot off?

Lamb kneels down and takes Josef's boot off.

LAMB: Okay, okay, I got it –

Lamb glances down; he gasps and recoils violently.

Hamilton looks at the foot and whips his head away, his hand over his mouth.

LAMB: Did you see that!?

Hamilton groans.

LAMB: What the fuck!?

HAMILTON: I think ... (*looks again, turns back*) It must be an infection / of some sort. I don't know.

LAMB: Jesus fucking Christ.

JOSEF: Hey!

Josef indicates the other boot: he wants it off.

LAMB: Are you serious?

HAMILTON: It probably hurts like hell.

Hamilton goes over and removes the boot.

LAMB: *(glances at the other foot)* Oh *fuck.*

Hamilton turns to look at Lamb.

HAMILTON: Inspector ... !

LAMB: Yeah. I'll call an ambulance.

With Lamb looking away, Josef implores Hamilton to help him.

HAMILTON: It'll be faster if I drive him.

LAMB: I'll let them know you're coming.

HAMILTON: Good idea.

Lamb picks up his desk phone and dials out. During the phone call, Hamilton puts his coat over Josef's shoulder and guides him toward the door. It's a slow, laborious process.

LAMB: Chris? Put me through to emerg at East General. (...) Hi, this is Inspector Lamb of 56 Division. (...) Yeah. I've got a John Doe on his way over to you, with a serious foot infection or something. He'll be there in five, ten minutes. (...) Yes. He'll be with a lawyer, Hamilton Barnes. (...) Yes. (...) Thank you. *(hangs up)*
They're waiting for you.

HAMILTON: Great. Give me your card and I'll call you when he's being seen.

LAMB: *(taken aback by the request, pats his pockets)* Uh ... Shit. I don't have any on me ...

Hamilton isn't listening; he's helping Josef, who can barely walk. Every step is painful.

LAMB: I'll call you in an hour, okay? You can let me know –

There's a loud knock at the door. The three men freeze. The door opens.

ELENA *enters. She's dripping wet from the rain outside, and the small umbrella in her hand is twisted from the wind. She has a small backpack slung over her shoulder and wears pale blue scrubs and jeans.*

LAMB: Can I help you?

Elena looks at Lamb, surprised.

ELENA: Didn't you call for an interpreter?

HALF-LIGHT.

FIRST INTERLUDE

The sound of cellos rises into the air. Curious. Questioning.

SCENE 2

Lights up.

A first-aid kit is open on the desk. Josef is seated, Hamilton's coat still draped over his shoulders. Elena, wearing latex gloves, examines his feet. Hamilton and Lamb stand a little further off.

ELENA: Well. That's quite something.

LAMB: Told ya.

Elena turns Josef's foot. He winces in pain.

HAMILTON: I'm confused. Are you a nurse or a translator?

ELENA: Nurse, but I'm also on the roster of police interpreters. (*turns to Hamilton*) Not exactly a lot of Lavinians in the city. (*turns back to Josef's feet*) You're lucky you caught me at the end of my shift.

LAMB: Yeah. Makes you believe in Christmas miracles.

HAMILTON: What is it, some kind of toenail infection?

ELENA: It doesn't look infected ... The wound is surprisingly clean, actually. And just so you know, he doesn't have any toenails. They've been pulled out.

*HAMILTON: What?

*LAMB: Like out, out?

ELENA: (*snaps her gloves off*) Yeah.

LAMB: Jesus ...

HAMILTON: Was he tortured?

ELENA: That'd be my guess.

LAMB: Christ.

HAMILTON: (*to Lamb*) I can still take him to the hospital.

ELENA: You're next of kin?

HAMILTON: (*shakes his head*) You don't think he needs to see a doctor?

ELENA: Of course he does. But he shouldn't be walking anywhere. (*to Lamb*) I can call an ambulance.

LAMB: Yeah, please.

Elena takes out her phone and dials a number.

HAMILTON: I can drive him over –

ELENA: It's too dangerous for him to walk. (*to Lamb*) Can we put his feet up? He'll be more comfortable –
　　　(*into phone*) Hello? (*turns away*)

LAMB: (*to Hamilton*) You can be a lot of things in a police station, but comfortable ain't one of 'em.

Lamb brings over a chair to elevate Josef's feet. He goes to move Josef's legs, but glimpses the toes again and turns away.

ELENA: Twenty, twenty-five minutes.

Elena comes over to help lift Josef's legs up on the chair.

HAMILTON: That long?

As Josef's legs are shifted, Hamilton's coat slips off his shoulders.

ELENA: He's not in critical danger.

LAMB: I'd like to ask him a few questions.

ELENA: Of course.

HAMILTON: (*to Lamb*) Don't you think he's been interrogated enough?

Elena notices Josef's uniform and epaulettes.

LAMB: Just 'cause he can't walk the walk doesn't mean he can't talk the ... (*off Hamilton's look*) Oh, that was really ... I'm sorry. (*to Elena*) It's a form of Tourette's. (*notices her interest in the uniform*) Miss?

ELENA: This uniform ... Where did you find him?

LAMB: Two kids dropped him off at the station, why?

ELENA: It's a Sužni uniform. (*points to the epaulettes*) Rank of general.

LAMB: General? (*to Josef*) Didn't mean to demote you to sergeant, friend.

ELENA: This isn't a joke.

LAMB: Sorry?

ELENA: A Sužni general, Inspector. That's like someone walking in here dressed in a Nazi uniform –

HAMILTON: A *Nazi* uniform?

LAMB: Okay, whoa whoa whoa. Why do I feel like the odd man out here? (*to Hamilton*) You know what she's talking about?

HAMILTON: I just think comparing a civil war to the Third Reich / is a bit much.

ELENA: (*to Hamilton*) Jaste li Lavinijanac?

HAMILTON: I'm sorry?

ELENA: You're not from Lavinia?

HAMILTON: No.

ELENA: Not a lot of people know our country even exists, let alone our history.

LAMB: Yeah, but this guy's like Google in real life.

ELENA: And there's nothing civil about genocide.

HAMILTON: Look, I ... I wasn't trying to – I'm not an expert, by any means. I read *The Economist*. And I have a colleague who's from there who explained it to me once, and he called it a civil war.

ELENA: I bet he did.

LAMB: But y'all speak the same language, right?

ELENA: As hard as it may be to believe, yes.

LAMB: So the uniform is from the war?

Elena nods.

LAMB: (*flips through his notes*) Okay. What does this mean? 'Ne-chu-vi-nicho-rachi'?

ELENA: Sounds like, 'I won't tell you anything.'

LAMB: Guess that bears out the torture theory. Ask him for his name.

ELENA: Kato se zavite? (*beat*) Voše nime? (*beat*) Not the talkative type, I guess.

LAMB: Gosh, I'm glad we waited for a translator.
Ask him if he knows the two kids who brought him in.

ELENA: Ko su bili ljumi koi su vas davili vodje?

JOSEF: Njima vaza.

ELENA: He says he doesn't know.

LAMB: Tell him we want to help him, but we need to know who he is first.

ELENA: Čilemo vam pomači ali berta nam voše nime.

JOSEF: Maje nime ne vezi.

ELENA: He doesn't want to say his name.

JOSEF: Ne vjirujem da mi čilete pomači ni tsikand. Znomam vodole ste.

LAMB: What'd he say?

ELENA: He doesn't believe I want to help him.

HAMILTON: That's all he said?

Elena and Lamb turn to Hamilton.

ELENA: Yes, why?

HAMILTON: Just seemed like there was more than that.

LAMB: How long has he been in Canada?

ELENA: Kaleto dago ste je vodje?

JOSEF: Ka je voše sojnime?

ELENA: He's asking me if I'm a Sužni or Desni.

LAMB: Those are the two ethnic groups?

Elena nods.

LAMB: Let me guess: he's Sužni, and you're ...

ELENA: *(looks at Josef)* Desni.

JOSEF: *(stands up)* Kurvetino!

Josef spits at Elena's feet. She takes a step back.

*LAMB: What the ... ?

*HAMILTON: Whoa!

Lamb shoves Josef back to his seat.

LAMB: Christ. I won't have any of that. D'you hear? I won't have you
threatening people.
    (to Elena) I'm sorry about that. He hasn't been violent at all.

ELENA: It's fine.

LAMB: I don't like this sudden change in attitude.

HAMILTON: It may be a mental health issue ...

LAMB: I don't get the sense he's cray-cray. *(off Hamilton's look)* My daughter
says that.

ELENA: If we believe what his uniform says –

HAMILTON: You're assuming it's his.

LAMB: It fits him perfectly.

ELENA: You understand that *every* high-ranking Sužni officer is wanted by Interpol? If he's one –

LAMB: Now hold on, just because he's wearing a uniform –

ELENA: There's a tattoo, as well.

*HAMILTON: Excuse me?

*LAMB: Say again?

ELENA: All Sužni officers have a tattoo above their heart. (*puts her hand above her heart*) Cerberus holding a knife.

Lamb looks at Hamilton. Hamilton cocks his head, as if to say, 'Seriously?'

LAMB: (*to Hamilton*) Look, if it's not there ...

ELENA: If it's not there, I won't say another word about it.

LAMB: Can you ask him to unbutton his jacket?

HAMILTON: The legality of all this is ... questionable.
(*off Lamb's look*) I'm just saying. Once a lawyer, always a lawyer.

Lamb nods to Elena.

ELENA: Raskomajte plaknu.

LAMB: Please.

ELENA: Nalim vas.

Josef looks at Elena, then Lamb, and finally Hamilton. He begins to unbutton his jacket.

LAMB: What's a cerberus?

ELENA: It's a three-headed dog.

LAMB: Right. Let me guess. Latin?

ELENA: Greek, I think.

LAMB: Whatever happened to plain old English?

Josef opens his jacket. Above his heart is a large tattoo of a cerberus holding a knife in its right paw.

ELENA: It's tattooed over the heart so they never lose courage in battle.

LAMB: I'm wishing I'd stayed home for this shift.

HAMILTON: Now hold on. (*to Elena*) You're saying this old man is ... what, exactly?

ELENA: The uniform, the tattoo, the *attitude* ...

HAMILTON: Yes?

ELENA: (*to Lamb*) All I know is that high-ranking Sužni officers are wanted for war crimes.

LAMB: Yeah, but he's an old man.

ELENA: The war was twenty-two years ago.

LAMB: Oh. (*looks at Josef*) Christ.

ELENA: I don't know, can't you look it up on the Interpol database or whatever?

HAMILTON: I thought you were an expert.

LAMB: I don't have access here, I'd have to – (*waves toward the door*) Look, I got two kids waiting for me at home, so please, don't make me go on a wild goose chase ...

ELENA: I don't know *exactly* who he is, okay? But there's only a handful of people he could be ... Gnivomír Ilić, the Black Wolf? Juraj Plamen? Kazimir Mstijov, the Red / Knight? Josef Džibrilovo, the Butcher?

HAMILTON: (*to Lamb*) This is getting us nowhere.

LAMB: Wait, what was that last one?

ELENA: Josef Džibrilovo?

LAMB: His nickname?

ELENA: The Butcher.

Lamb looks at Hamilton.

ELENA: What?

Lamb goes to his desk and takes out the butcher's hook.

LAMB: It was around his neck.

Elena looks at it, then turns to Josef.

ELENA: Sonofabitch.

HAMILTON: Now hold on. *Anyone* could have put that around his neck and dressed him up in that uniform. Everything you're saying is circumstantial. (*to Lamb*) You can't convict a man over a piece of ... jewellery.

Lamb and Elena look at Hamilton.

LAMB: Look, I don't know what's what, but you may be out of your depth here, Mr. Barnes. Maybe we should get this gentleman a real lawyer.

ELENA: I thought you were a / lawyer.

*LAMB: He's a copyright lawyer.

*HAMILTON: Well, yes.

ELENA: What is a copyright lawyer doing here?

HAMILTON: I don't answer / to you.

LAMB: He had his business card on him.

ELENA: How do you know him?

HAMILTON: I don't!

ELENA: So he just *happened* to have your business card?

LAMB: Yeah, we kinda went through this already.

HAMILTON: (*to Elena*) I don't like your tone.

ELENA: I don't care if you do or don't.

LAMB: So much for the Christmas spirit, then.

ELENA: This isn't funny!

LAMB: Miss, at this point I ain't gonna be home with my kids until the new year because of the paperwork this entire effing evening is gonna generate. So trust me when I say, I ain't laughing.

ELENA: Don't you realize who you have here?

LAMB: I don't know anything, actually. There's no proof of anything / in terms of this man's identity.

HAMILTON: Exactly!

ELENA: You think this is all, what? A fluke?

HAMILTON: All we *know* is that he's an old man who's –

ELENA: I want to know who he was twenty years ago.

HAMILTON: Does it mean nothing to you that he's been tortured?

ELENA: Of course. But why do *you* care so much about a guy you've never seen before?

HAMILTON: I'm a lawyer.

ELENA: But you're not his lawyer.

LAMB: The question's been bugging me too, Mr. Barnes.

HAMILTON: Look. I appreciate that you're a nurse-translator-whatever, no offence, but in the short span of time you've been here he's gone from being a victim to a war criminal.

ELENA: Ne vjirujem vim. Ve ste Lavinijanac.

LAMB: What is she saying?

HAMILTON: I've no idea.

JOSEF: Talči, kurvetino.

LAMB: Wait, what is he saying?

ELENA: Nothing nice.

HAMILTON: I'm sorry, but you can't go around accusing someone of being a war criminal! It's a matter of principle.

ELENA: You're right.

HAMILTON: Right ... Well ... There you go.

ELENA: This could just be some guy, who *happens* to speak Lavinian, who *happens* to be wearing a general's uniform, who *happens* to have the Sužni tattoo, and who *happens* to be wearing a butcher's hook. (*beat*) Wouldn't want to jump to any conclusions.

HAMILTON: I'm sure these arguments all make sense in your head. But from a legal standpoint, it's all hearsay and conjecture.

Elena and Hamilton glare at each other.

ELENA: Let's Google him. Džibrilovo.

LAMB: That's an idea.

Lamb goes to the computer on his desk.

LAMB: Okay.

ELENA: D-Ž-I-B-R-

LAMB: Slow down.

ELENA: D-Ž-I-B-R-I-L-O-V-O.

LAMB: Not exactly a phonetic language, is it? (*beat*) Josef Dzee ... What she said. Known as the Butcher. (*looks at Hamilton*) She's not making that part up.

ELENA: Are there photographs of him?

LAMB: Hold on ... (*beat*) Well fuck me.

ELENA: It looks like him, doesn't it?

LAMB: Nope.

*ELENA: What!?

*HAMILTON: See?

ELENA: (*to Lamb*) It doesn't?

LAMB: I'm sorry. It doesn't look like him. (*points to Hamilton*) It looks like him.

HAMILTON: ... What?

Lamb turns the screen to show Elena and Hamilton.

ELENA: Hello.

Lamb and Elena turn to Hamilton.

HAMILTON: The features are similar, I'll grant you ...

ELENA: *Similar?*

HAMILTON: Look, yes, okay? It looks a little bit like me ... (*off Lamb's look*) It's not ... That's not so crazy if you take into account that my family's from Lavinia.

LAMB: So you lied to me?

HAMILTON: No, I didn't lie –

LAMB: You said your parents were from Birmingham.

HAMILTON: My adoptive parents, yes.

LAMB: Oh. So you weren't, de facto, lying?

HAMILTON: I left the country when I was very young.

LAMB: You're related to him?

HAMILTON: We're third or fourth cousins, something like that. I met him once when I was a kid, I think.

LAMB: So this is Josef Dzee-bree ...

ELENA: Džibrilovo.

HAMILTON: (*nods*) Yes.

Lamb exhales.

HAMILTON: Look, I don't think that he's –

ELENA: Don't you dare!

HAMILTON: Let me finish!

ELENA: I will *not* if it's –

HAMILTON: Will you shut up?

LAMB: You two are giving me a headache. (*to Elena*) Let him finish, will you?

HAMILTON: All I'm saying is that, I know he was a soldier in the war. I don't know if he was high-ranking or / not, but –

ELENA: A general, actually.

HAMILTON: Well, maybe. That's not my point.

ELENA: (*to Lamb*) He ran a concentration camp, where –

HAMILTON: Allegedly.

ELENA: Excuse me?

HAMILTON: He's accused of that crime, not convicted of it.

ELENA: Spoken as a true patriot.

HAMILTON: Spoken as a lawyer, actually.

ELENA: And was it as a lawyer that you were so insistent on driving him to the hospital yourself? (*beat*) I don't think you'd've ever seen them again, Inspector.

LAMB: Is that true?

HAMILTON: It is not. He's in danger here.

*LAMB: Here?

*ELENA: In a police station?

HAMILTON: There is a group of, of, people, they call themselves the *Fjurioji*, the Furies.

JOSEF: Da!

Everyone turns to Josef.

JOSEF: Fjurioji su me krobeli vu Buenos Airesu. Ti kači su me lošisilovli djejnima, vendjeljama, ne sačam se.

LAMB: What's he saying?

Elena opens her mouth to speak –

HAMILTON: That he was kidnapped and tortured –

Lamb and Elena turn to Hamilton.

LAMB: You and I are going to have a long chat about your definition of 'truth.'

Hamilton puts up his hands, apologetic.

HAMILTON: I was scared for him, okay? The *Fjurioji*? They're a death squad that tracks down Sužni leaders.

LAMB: So they're the ones who dropped him off here?

HAMILTON: That's what doesn't make sense. When the *Fjurioji* catch you, they kill you. They aren't interested in justice. They want revenge. (*indicates Josef*) He shouldn't be alive. They've never let anyone go. Or handed anyone over to be tried.

　　(*to Josef*) What did they ask you? Ted su voni – (*to Elena*) What's the word for 'interrogate'?

ELENA: Vispitevati.

HAMILTON: (*to Josef*) Ted su te voni vispitevali, što su te voni dečeli tebi?

JOSEF: Vaj?

ELENA: Šta su vas jaskali?

*HAMILTON: I'm rusty.

*JOSEF: Oh! Ne znonam zar, ali jaskali su o nošim kodstanu, Juriju. Mož su čili, da ga mestu –

ELENA: (*to Lamb*) Hold on. He just said, 'They were asking about *our* neighbour, Yuri.'

HAMILTON: Yes, but he's not finished –

LAMB: (*to Elena*) That's an exact translation?

ELENA: Word for word.

LAMB: Mr. Barnes, one more lie from you and I will arrest you for obstruction.

HAMILTON: Okay, wait – I'm confused ...

LAMB: *Our* neighbour. Not *my* neighbour. *Our.* Meaning you both lived in the same house.

HAMILTON: I'm sure it was just a —

LAMB: Nah-uh. The whole cousin thing wasn't really jiving for me anyways. He's what, your father? Your uncle?

Hamilton looks at Josef.

HAMILTON: Father.

Lamb and Elena exchange a glance.

ELENA: I thought his two children died in a car accident before the war.

HAMILTON: My mother and sister did. They bought a corpse at the morgue and passed it off as my own. I was shipped off to England. (*looks at Josef*) I was told he was dead. This is the first time I've seen him in twenty-five years.

LAMB: Merry Christmas. (*awkward*) Or whatever. (*takes Hamilton's business card*) I guess someone figured it was time for a family reunion.

HAMILTON: (*to himself*) Of course.

LAMB: What?

HAMILTON: Yuri. They were asking him about Yuri. He was my 'fixer,' and the only person who knows ... (*to Josef*) Jasi li nim račao po Yuriju?

JOSEF: (*nods*) Ašto?

HAMILTON: Von je jadini koj znoma moe nime!

Josef takes in this information, then suddenly takes a sharp intake of breath.

JOSEF: (*points to Hamilton*) Ti! Baže te!

Hamilton rushes over to Lamb.

Elena takes her phone from its belt clip, dials a number and returns the phone to her belt clip.

*HAMILTON: Inspector, I need your help, you have to protect me!

*JOSEF: Oprasi mi, oprasi mi, ja som gniv ...

LAMB: Okay, calm down, what the hell is going on?

HAMILTON: The *Fjurioji*, they're not looking for him. They're looking for me!

LAMB: Friend, you're in a police station, take it easy –

HAMILTON: No, that doesn't matter, they're – you don't understand who you're dealing with!

LAMB: Okay, okay, slow down –

JOSEF: Daži vadovde! Brči!

HAMILTON: He's right, I have to get out of here –

ELENA: Niko ne odvidje nidje.

Josef and Hamilton freeze.

LAMB: What?

ELENA: I said, no one's going anywhere.
(*to Hamilton*) We wanted to be 100 percent sure, of course, but now that you've confirmed it ...
It's a pleasure to finally meet you, Marko Džibrilovo.

Elena smiles.

HALF-LIGHT.

SECOND INTERLUDE

The sound of the cellos rise into the air. Hungry. Threatening.

SCENE 3

Lights up.

Hamilton is on the ground, writhing in pain. Elena has him in a wristlock.

Josef, now standing, watches. Lamb points his gun at Elena.

JOSEF: Šukaj je!

LAMB: Miss, I'm gonna ask you one last time –

Elena releases Hamilton. He scrambles to his feet and joins Josef and Lamb. Elena stands by the door, unfazed by the gun pointed at her.

LAMB: Now I want you to turn around and –

ELENA: Gentlemen. There seems to be some confusion about who has the upper hand here.

LAMB: I'll say. Now, for the last time –

ELENA: June 13th, 2001.

Lamb frowns.

ELENA: May 3rd, 2007.

LAMB: Those dates ... How ... ?

HAMILTON: What's wrong with you?

LAMB: Those are my kids' birthdays ...

Hamilton whips his head back to Elena.

ELENA: Erin Lamb, Grade Eight at Courcelette Public School. Her best subject is math and she's partial to red shoes.

Iris is in the first grade and her best friend is a shy Korean girl named Sunny. She was over last weekend and made chocolate chip cookies, isn't that right?

Lamb is dazed.

ELENA: So you see, this isn't amateur hour.

> Lower your gun, Inspector.

Lamb doesn't move.

ELENA: Danijel.

From Elena's phone comes a thickly accented voice.

DANIJEL (O.S.): Da?

ELENA: Tell Inspector Lamb where you and your men are parked right now.

DANIJEL (O.S.): We are in front of one-oh-nine Grandview Street. Pine tree in yard is decorate with blue lights.

Lamb lowers his gun.

ELENA: You are not the target, Inspector. (*indicates her phone*) My colleague is listening, and as long as you do as I say and Danijel continues to hear my voice, neither your daughters nor your wife will be harmed. You have my word. (*holds out her hand*) Your gun, please.

Lamb takes a step toward Elena.

HAMILTON: Don't do this.

LAMB: I'm sorry ... But ...

HAMILTON: *Please.*

LAMB: This is my *family.*

Lamb goes to Elena and hands her his gun.

ELENA: Lock the door.

Lamb takes out his key ring and locks the door.

ELENA: (*puts her hand out*) Keys.

Lamb gives them to her. Elena checks the door; it's locked. No one can get out.

ELENA: Take my backpack.

Lamb obeys.

ELENA: Put your phones in there, both of you.

Lamb does as he's told. Hamilton doesn't move.

ELENA: Take it from him, Inspector.

Lamb goes to Hamilton and pats his pockets. Lamb finds Hamilton's phone and puts it in the backpack.

Elena extends her hand; Lamb gives the backpack back to her.

ELENA: (*points to desk phone*) Unplug that phone.

Lamb does as he's told.

ELENA: Now. One of you may be tempted to yell for help or call attention to our little get-together. Let me be clear: the only result of such action will be that everyone in this room – and at 109 Grandview – will die. Understood? (*beat*) Understood?

Lamb nods.

Hamilton nods.

ELENA: Good. We can keep this civilized, can't we?

Elena takes out the clip from Lamb's gun, puts the clip in her pocket, then puts the gun in the back of her jeans.

She indicates a chair for Hamilton. Lamb and Josef look at Hamilton. He sits down in the chair.

HAMILTON: What do you want?

ELENA: It's not what I want, Marko, it's what we want. I represent the interests of many people here.

JOSEF: Pretsao som ti, da je vona stavno varljava kurvetina.

ELENA: Don't call me that.

    (*off Lamb's look*) He calls me a *kurvetina*. It translates as 'bog donkey,' but in Lavinian it means something like a cunty whore.

    A wonderfully progressive people, as you can see.

HAMILTON: Your soldiers urinate on enemy corpses. Like dogs marking their territory.

ELENA: Do we? Why yes, I suppose we do. But we would like to take exception to something you said earlier, about how we seek only revenge, and not justice. That is not true. We seek both.

    Your mistake is thinking that there is a difference.

HAMILTON: That's a fine bit of sophistry, but –

ELENA: Does it make you feel better to use words no one understands?

HAMILTON: All I mean –

ELENA: I don't care what you mean. We've heard the arguments, and they are always the same.

    We tried to do it your way, you know. During the peace talks, we submitted a list of fourteen officers we wanted tried for war crimes. The West agreed, but the Sužni brokered a secret deal with them to let the officers leave the country. Because nothing, you see, would be allowed to derail the 'peace process.'

    We learned our lesson.

    Let me ask you a question, Marko: if you take away the scales of justice, what's left?

HAMILTON: Nothing.

ELENA: Wrong. She's left with her sword.

HAMILTON: ...

ELENA: Inspector, would you be so kind as to handcuff our friend here to the chair?

Hamilton rises. Elena makes a calming gesture.

ELENA: This may surprise you, Marko, but we are not interested in killing you. Your co-operation is expected, however, and force will be used if necessary. (*pats the chair*) Sit down.

Hamilton doesn't move. Elena goes to her backpack and takes out two zip ties.

LAMB: Please, do as she says ...

Lamb puts his hand on Hamilton's shoulder. Hamilton brushes him off. Lamb grabs him again, this time with a firmer grip.

LAMB: *Please.*

HAMILTON: (*puts up his hands in surrender*) Okay, okay.

Hamilton sits. Lamb cuffs his hands behind the chair.

LAMB: (*whispers*) Sorry.

ELENA: Tie his legs with these when you're done.

Elena throws a pair of zip ties to Lamb.

Lamb ties Hamilton's legs to the chair.

ELENA: Lest you find us unfair, we've decided to give your father a trial. We want him to confess to his crimes. Then together, you and I will agree on a suitable punishment.

HAMILTON: You've already found him guilty of his 'crimes.'

ELENA: Of course we have. But *you* haven't.
(*to Josef*) Čilimo da vespamjedate svoe zarčine sonu.

JOSEF: Jači se kurvetino.

ELENA: Such petulance.

HAMILTON: He's right. Why take part in your charade? You're going to kill us anyway.

ELENA: Quite the pessimist, aren't you? Everything depends on how co-operative your father is.

   (*to Josef*) Here's the deal, Butcher: confess your crimes to your son and submit to our punishment, and he will live.

LAMB: He doesn't speak English.

ELENA: Oh, but he understands it, Inspector. He's been a naughty boy, pretending not to all this time.

LAMB: I really don't think he –

ELENA: Stop being so naive. (*to Josef*) Now I suppose we can't have you confess *all* your crimes, we don't have that much time. So instead, there is one specific instance we want you to share, one sin that is indicative of ... (*turns to Hamilton*) Well, you'll see.

   There was, at his camp, one particular prisoner known as the Duchess. (*to Josef*) Vajvotinja.

Josef looks away.

ELENA: Oh, how touching. He remembers her.

Hamilton looks at Elena.

ELENA: She died in the camp. (*to Josef*) Tell your son what you did to her.

JOSEF: Ne.

LAMB: Sonofabitch understands English.

ELENA: Tell him.

JOSEF: Vinaće murčete i mani i njiga.

ELENA: Your death warrant was signed when we found you, Butcher. That's true. (*points to Hamilton*) But his remains ... unclear at the moment.

HAMILTON: He won't give in to your tyranny.

ELENA: (*laughs*) You hear that, Butcher? A proud man, your son. A *principled* man.

JOSEF: Dran te bilo, kurvetino!

ELENA: I told you not to call me that.

So, one last time. Tell your son what you did to the *Vajvotinja*.

Josef glares at Elena.

ELENA: All right. (*goes to her backpack and pulls out a sophisticated-looking mouth gag; to Josef*) Our own special design: a combination bite-stick and sound dampener. Ingenious, no?

HAMILTON: Confessions made under torture tend to be unreliable.

ELENA: Well of course they are. (*gives the gag to Lamb*) But they are much more reliable when the subject is forced to watch a family member being tortured.

Hamilton lets this sink in —

HAMILTON: (*struggles against his restraints*) HEL—

Elena grabs Hamilton by the throat and squeezes his windpipe.

ELENA: I thought we talked about shouting, Marko.

Elena releases Hamilton; he coughs, unable to speak.

ELENA: (*to Lamb*) Gag him.

LAMB: Don't do this.

ELENA: I'm not asking for advice.

LAMB: It's not right.

ELENA: Of course it's not *right*.

Now gag him before I make your family the unfortunate victims of a home invasion.

Elena's words puncture Lamb's courage.

Lamb goes over to Hamilton. Hamilton struggles, but Lamb is stronger and gets the gag into Hamilton's mouth.

ELENA: Good boy.

Lamb secures the gag in place.

ELENA: There were a lot of escape attempts when your father's camp first 'opened.' (*goes to the desk*) He needed a way to convince prisoners that such behaviour wasn't worth the risk. Executing prisoners was useless, since it was more of a blessing than being alive ...

Elena picks up the butcher's hook.

JOSEF: Nimajte ga odsrediti ...

ELENA: He needed a deterrent that was more permanent than beatings or simple torture. Now, to be fair? His solution was rather elegant, all things considered.
    (*raises the butcher's hook*) He severed one of their Achilles tendons. Captured escapees would have to crawl around the camp until they could walk again. And when they did, they *limped*.

JOSEF: Murčete me. Nekite ga vu miru.

ELENA: Vajvotinja?

JOSEF: Ne sačam se ...

ELENA: Liar. (*turns to Hamilton*) People with principles and integrity are the same as the captured escapees, Marko. Everyone admires them for their courage, but so few are willing to pay the price. Your father understood that.
    He had a nickname for them: *Solizgači*.
    It means 'those who grovel.'

Elena, hook in hand, steps toward Hamilton.

JOSEF: (*stands up*) Ne!

HALF-LIGHT.

THIRD INTERLUDE

The sound of the cellos rise into the air. Angry. Excruciating.

SCENE 4

Lights up.

Hamilton is passed out on the chair. His shoes and socks have been removed, and his left pant leg is rolled up. The gag hangs around his neck. His heel is expertly bandaged. The gauze is bloody.

Elena leans against a desk and watches Hamilton. Lamb sits at his desk, head bowed. Josef, slumped on the floor, mumbles to himself.

Elena goes over to Hamilton, looks into his face. She gently slaps him.

ELENA: Come on, Marko. You're a big boy now.

She crushes a pack of smelling salts and waves it under his nose.

Hamilton, woozy with pain, comes to.

ELENA: There you are.

Hamilton groans. Lamb fumbles in his pockets and pulls out a pill bottle.

LAMB: Can I?

ELENA: What?

LAMB: Aspirin.

ELENA: In a prescription bottle?

LAMB: ... OxyContin. (*off Elena's look*) I have arthritis.

ELENA: Uh-uh. No painkillers.

LAMB: But —

ELENA: No.

LAMB: I ... Please.

ELENA: No. I want him alert.

LAMB: He just *passed out* from the pain!

Elena shakes her head. Hamilton groans.

LAMB: I'm begging you. *One.*

ELENA: (*to Hamilton*) Would you look at that? A man you hardly know is begging on your behalf. You should feel special.
   (*to Lamb*) One.

Lamb nods. He looks around for water: nothing.

He goes to the wastebasket and pulls out Hamilton's unfinished coffee.

LAMB: Hey buddy ... Can you hear me?

Hamilton looks up at Lamb.

LAMB: Painkillers. They'll help, okay?

Lamb puts a pill into his palm, then quickly glances at Elena. He puts two more pills in his palm and brings them up to Hamilton's mouth. Hamilton accepts the pills. Lamb puts the coffee to Hamilton's lips and helps him drink.

HAMILTON: (*grimaces*) ... Thank you ...

Lamb pats Hamilton on the shoulder.

ELENA: Now that we're back ... Have you changed your mind, Butcher?

JOSEF: Šao mi je, Marko, šao mi je –

ELENA: I'm talking to you!

JOSEF: Zmejo! Grazna zmeja vod žine!

ELENA: Your son still has his right Achilles. You want to go through this again?

JOSEF: Ti si kurvetina, tvaja makica je bila kurvetina, i njina makica jesto je bila kurvetina –

ELENA: You are a pig-headed old man, aren't you?
   (*to Lamb*) Prepare the other foot.

LAMB: Please, no ...

Hamilton bursts into tears. Everyone looks at him.

Lamb turns away, embarrassed.

ELENA: *(to Josef)* Ah, such courage, such ... fortitude.

Elena goes to the desk and picks up the butcher's hook –

JOSEF: Okay! Okay! Defta. Raču vim ... Raču vim.

ELENA: Vajvotinja?

Josef nods.

ELENA: Good.

Josef looks at Hamilton.

JOSEF: Čilu da mu pakložete glasči.

ELENA: What?

JOSEF: Marko. Ne možu vim rači ako me glida.

ELENA: He wants you blindfolded. He can't tell you and look you in the eyes at the same time.

Hamilton looks at Josef.

Josef looks away.

ELENA: What the hell. There's a certain poetry to it. *(to Lamb)* Blindfold him.

LAMB: With what?

ELENA: I don't know. Your tie.

Lamb unknots his tie and blindfolds Hamilton.

LAMB: Too tight?

Hamilton shakes his head.

Elena comes up behind Hamilton and puts her hand on his shoulders. He flinches.

ELENA: (*to Josef*) Now, Butcher. Make sure you tell the truth, yes? Because if you don't … (*she squeezes Hamilton's shoulders*) Understood?

Josef nods.

ELENA: Say it.

JOSEF: Da, da, mnogo klarno. Ja kaću dovariti desnu.

ELENA: (*to Hamilton*) I'll translate to make sure you understan– (*stops; giggles*) I just had a better idea.

Marko. You're going to translate what he says. You may not see your father as he tells you his sins, but perhaps you can taste them.

Elena sits down.

ELENA: All right. You may confess, Butcher.

JOSEF: Bila je žina vu logru, seki ju je zonao Vajvotinja –

ELENA: Slow down so he can keep up.

*JOSEF: Bila je, bila je žina vu logru, seki ju je zonao Vajvotinja, jar je stilno nasela draljinu, purpurnu draljinu.

Bila je omašna, Zadstaneš? Ostalim zorabljicima dala je *doru*, i nema čuge kao dore.

Zonao som, zonao som da som marnao nju razbeniti, razbeniti je bez kabijanja.

Pazovano som dvenieset mojih vojneca ka sebe i tanio som Vajvotinju. Na sebi je vnesila purpurnu draljinu … Onstovio som pratore i barta tevarena, tako da seki vu logru je moganu šuti … Mi je vačemo za stalicu, otrinata prima dalje …

*HAMILTON: (*translates haltingly*) There was a, a prisoner in the camp, everyone called her the Duchess. Because she always wore a dress, a purple dress.

She was dangerous, you understand? She gave the other prisoners *hope*, and nothing is a threat like hope.

I knew that I had to break her, break her without killing her.

So I invited twelve of my men to my quarters and brought the Duchess there. She was wearing the purple dress ... I left the windows and the door open, so everyone in the camp could hear her ... We tied her to my desk, facing down ...

Hamilton stops, overwhelmed.

*JOSEF: I ... I moi moveci, jadin po jadin je selaju. Pronekad je bilo dvaje vo jastavrime, pronekad traje.

*HAMILTON: And my men ... one by ...

As Josef continues his story, Hamilton attempts to translate. He mouths a few words here and there, but no sound comes out.

JOSEF: Padrinuo som se da nekaliku od njih je jazmu vu ... od obrodi. Pretsao som vojnece da usiparne, ali to je podzelo taško jer je ona otkarvela iz ... odesad. S njekih nije bilo barga, ali nekima je bilo gramljivo ... Jas som ih prešalio, naordio im da zakanaše ... Upala je vu neznavest, ali karestili sne reašljave sali jer mi je bilo zatrabno da vrešti, da nas mali da otprestenamo.

I kad su otvečeli moi moveci, bio je moj tran. I preradio som da je vodvažu – vu venom tanotku bila je prevaniše odiskrepljena da se odbrači – padrinuo som se da je volukam vu glasči kad som je udabio.

Vonda som naordio da seki odzimne šineve –

ELENA: Ne.

Josef looks at Elena.

ELENA: After you ... finished. You told her to say something to everyone.

Josef stares at Elena. She removes Hamilton's blindfold.

ELENA: What did you tell her to say to the soldiers after you were all done with her?

Josef stares at Elena, then looks away.

JOSEF: Vola.

Broken, Hamilton shakes his head.

ELENA: And then you ordered your soldiers to take out their knives and ...

JOSEF: ... i naordio som da seki izmerkeže njen žotrb. Po jadin strikar seki.

ELENA: ... and had them mark her stomach. One notch each.

Hamilton turns away from his father, disgusted.

Elena lifts up her shirt. There are thirteen stretched-out knife scars on her stomach.

ELENA: Then you patted me on the head and said, 'You earned your stripes, *kurvetino*.'

HAMILTON: That can't ... You would've been a, a *child* ...

Hamilton turns to his father.

ELENA: It was rather shrewd of your father not to mention her *age*.

JOSEF: Prekla si da je omrtvana.

ELENA: It's true, the *Vajvotinja* died in that camp ... Whoever I was before that night, she has never come back. Now I am just an instrument, Butcher. (*to Hamilton*) Do you see, now, Marko?

Hamilton looks away.

ELENA: You're right. There are no *words*. (*beat*) So what do we do with him now?

HAMILTON: You should – (*about to say 'kill'*)

ELENA: Yes?

HAMILTON: ... hand him over to Interpol. He should be tried in a court of law.

ELENA: Marko, Marko, Marko. I had such high hopes for you. Yet you cling to these outdated notions of ... (*sighs*)

Fine. Let us, for the sake of argument, accept that we hand him over to the ICC. He will be tried for war crimes, yes? For crimes against humanity? (*beat*) How long, in your professional opinion, would his trial take?

Hamilton shrugs.

ELENA: Ballpark it.

HAMILTON: A few years ...

ELENA: Two, three?

HAMILTON: Yes.

ELENA: Four, five? *Ten?*

HAMILTON: ... Maybe, yes.

ELENA: So he'll be eighty by the time he is convicted? And sentenced to, what? Life?

Hamilton nods.

ELENA: So they will send this eighty-year-old man to live out the rest of his life in a facility where he'll have access to first-rate medical care and cable television.

This, to you, is justice?

Hamilton looks at Elena.

ELENA: How can you sit there and tell me, *me*, that this man deserves a fair trial, deserves to be treated with dignity? He has *confessed*, his guilt is not in question, and you yourself seem to agree that the crime is heinous ...

HAMILTON: If you kill him, you become the very thing you are trying to destroy ...

ELENA: Why do you insist on speaking the language of civilization in a world that has seen so little of it? (*beat*) Do you even understand what revenge is, Marko? It is the confession of pain. Not whispered to a priest, but bellowed for the world to hear. Why? Because it is generous: it wants you to feel what it feels. And unlike you, it speaks a language everyone can understand: fairness and hate.

That is why I am not *satisfied* when you say to me, 'He must be tried in a court of law.'

So I ask you again: what is the just penalty for his crimes?

HAMILTON: You won't kill him with my blessing.

ELENA: Thankfully we did not go through all this trouble for your *blessing*.

Don't you think our revenge should equal the, the *ingenuity* of your father's crimes?

Hamilton looks up at Elena.

ELENA: (*removes her belt*) To kill the Butcher is easy.

But to have him executed by his own son ... ?

Well now, that is ... *elegant.*

Hamilton shakes his head.

ELENA: You will strangle him with this belt.

I should warn you that it'll take several minutes to kill him. It's not as quick as the movies lead you to believe, I'm afraid.

HAMILTON: I won't do it.

ELENA: No?

HAMILTON: No.

JOSEF: Viži, kurvetino? Ne / kačeš –

HAMILTON: Stop calling her that! Have you no shame?

ELENA: Such chivalry, Marko.

HAMILTON: And you … Do you think you're so different than him?

ELENA: *(to Lamb)* Remove his handcuffs.

Lamb goes behind Hamilton and removes the handcuffs.

ELENA: His legs too.

Elena hands Lamb a pair of small wire cutters.

Lamb cuts the zip ties around Hamilton's legs.

HAMILTON: Threaten me, torture me all you want. I won't do it.

Lamb returns the wire cutters to Elena.

ELENA: Do you think, when we planned this, that we said, 'And when we tell him to kill his father, he'll do it?' *(shakes her head)* You're a good man, Marko, a good and honest man who would willingly sacrifice himself at the altar of justice. I respect that. There's even a part of me that admires that.

 So don't worry. *(gives belt to Hamilton)* We're going to help you.
 (goes over to the radiator) Inspector. *(puts out her hand)* Your handcuffs.

Lamb joins her and gives her his handcuffs.

ELENA: Key.

He hands it to her.

ELENA: Kneel.

LAMB: What?

ELENA: On your knees. Don't make me ask you again.

Lamb kneels down.

LAMB: Please don't kill me …

Elena handcuffs Lamb's wrists around a radiator pipe. Lamb is now in a stress position.

LAMB: Please ... !

ELENA: It's to protect you from yourself, Inspector. Trust me.
(*to Hamilton*) So now, Marko.

HAMILTON: You can rationalize all night long, I –

ELENA: Shh, shh, shh! The Furies must be satisfied. If I cannot offer
them your father ... (*shrugs*) Then I must offer them someone else.
Someone pure. Someone innocent.
Perhaps a thirteen-year-old girl? Or better yet, her seven-year-old
sister?

Lamb starts. The handcuffs rattle against the pipe.

LAMB: What!? No ... But ... Wait, I've noth– She's got nothing to
do with ...

ELENA: Oh, I know. I know. (*indicates Hamilton*) It's up to him, really.

Lamb looks at Hamilton.

HAMILTON: Oh God ...

LAMB: Mr. Barnes ... Hamilton ...

HAMILTON: Dear God ...

LAMB: My daughter ... But ... She's ... Iris ... ! (*looks at Elena*) I'll kill him.
I'll do it.

ELENA: No. It has to be him.

LAMB: Please ... Hamilton ... (*turns to Elena and pulls hard on the handcuffs*)
I will kill you, do you understand that? I will kill you if you hurt one
hair –

ELENA: *Inspector*. The reason I haven't gagged you is that I want you to
have the opportunity to beg for her life, understood?

Lamb nods, aware of his precarious position.

LAMB: Please, I'm begging you ... Not my daughters. They're ... They're *children*, they're innocent ...

ELENA: (*points to Hamilton*) You're asking the wrong person.

HAMILTON: Don't ...

LAMB: Hamilton ... You spoke to her, she's just a ... She's a ...

HAMILTON: This is wrong. This is all wrong.

*ELENA: Depends on your perspective.

*LAMB: I know, but Iris ... My little girl, Hamilton ...

HAMILTON: (*drops the belt*) No. This isn't right ... No.

LAMB: Wha ... ? Hamilton ... He ... What are you *saying*?

HAMILTON: I'm sorry ...

LAMB: Don't ... No ... (*to Elena*) Please. Please don't hurt them. Please ...

ELENA: Vu prosiciju i čikajte moj nišak, seg.

Elena places the phone on the corner of the desk so that Lamb and Hamilton can hear it better.

From the phone's speaker comes the sound of four car doors opening then closing, followed by footsteps in the rain.

DANIJEL (O.S.): Gotreman, seg.

ELENA: They're standing by.

LAMB: Hamilton ... I don't understand ... You said yourself that he wasn't going to leave this room alive ... What difference does it make? Iris ... Please ... Iris ... She's *seven* ... She's just –

ELENA: Marko?

HAMILTON: Please, have some compassion, some humanity ...

ELENA: I'm sorry, we do not speak the language of mercy.

Elena turns to her phone.

LAMB: No no no, wait, wait, let me talk to him some more –

ELENA: (*into her phone*) Vukapsite, seg.

HAMILTON: Please ...

DANIJEL (O.S.): Radio tašina, seg.

From the phone's speakers come the muffled sounds of a home invasion: lock picking, door opening, footsteps climbing stairs, more doors opening, voices quickly stifled, shuffling.

LAMB (*pleads softly as the invasion plays out*): Hamilton ... I'm begging you ... please ... my family ... Iris ... she's a child ... please ...

Then, silence.

DANIJEL (O.S.): Gošani provideni, seg.

ELENA: They're waiting for the kill order. Would you like to give it?

HAMILTON: Stop it ...

ELENA: Puvi najdjovenu na fonče.

Some jostling is heard coming from the phone, and then the tremulous voice of a young girl:

IRIS (O.S.): Daddy ...? Are you there ...?

LAMB: I'm right here, Pumpkin ... everything'll be okay ...

Lamb rattles his handcuffs.

ELENA: Defta.

The voice is cut off.

ELENA: I will give the kill order next, Marko.

How many bodies will it take for you to execute a dead man? Because we'll go through this again with Erin, and then Carol, and then our own Inspec–

HAMILTON: Okay. Okay. Don't harm her.

ELENA: Yes?

HAMILTON: You win.

ELENA: Čikaj za podatne vugrade, seg.

DANIJEL (O.S.): Zadstaneš, seg.

ELENA: *(to Lamb)* They're holding for the moment. But don't go thanking him until he's done the deed, Inspector.
(to Hamilton) Marko.

HAMILTON: Oprasmi, tače.

Hamilton picks up the belt.

ELENA: That warms my heart.

Josef goes to Hamilton and stops a few steps from him.

JOSEF: Pogradem se na tebe, sone. Jimena taleko malo mene vu tebi.

ELENA: That's very touching but –

JOSEF: Talči. Bíću olordar svojih lašjednih menata.

ELENA: No, Butcher. I am the master of your last minutes.
Now be a good father to your son, and teach him to kill you properly.

Josef glares at Elena, then turns to Hamilton.

JOSEF: Znomaš li kako ovo unaraditi?

HAMILTON: *(shakes his head)* Navorno da ne.

As Josef speaks to Hamilton, Elena uncuffs Lamb from the radiator.

JOSEF: Maračeš otstenuti moje lokarče lokenima.

Onda zabataj ramiš onako svoje najstrače lokarce. Dva tupa ako mačeniš.

Koda povačeš, nemoj vrepastiti. Nemoj vrepastiti. Zadstaneš?

Hamilton nods.

Elena goes to the desk and takes the mouth gag.

JOSEF: (*to Elena*) Gotreman som.

ELENA: (*throws gag at Lamb*) Gag him.

JOSEF: Ne barta mi.

ELENA: Nisom pretala.

Lamb comes over and gags Josef, then retreats to his desk.

Elena looks at Josef. He stands straight, ready.

ELENA: Look at him, Marko.

His poise, his dignity in his last moments.

He's probably thinking to himself that, all things considered, this is a good way to die.

Elena steps into Josef's personal space.

ELENA: That he has managed, despite everything, to maintain a shred of honour in his death.

Josef looks out, unmoved by Elena's words.

Elena whispers into Josef's ear.

Before Josef can react, Elena pushes him down onto his back.

ELENA: (*to Hamilton*) Get on with it.

Hamilton painfully kneels on Josef, so his back is to the audience (and we cannot see Josef being strangled). Hamilton grabs both ends of the belt and pins Josef's arms with his knees.

HAMILTON: Šao mi je ...

Hamilton pulls on the belt, with a kind of animal ferocity that takes everyone by surprise.

It will, in fact, take between two and three minutes for Josef to die.

The moment Hamilton begins to strangle his father, the sound of three cellos rises through the air. It's a dissonant cacophony that fragments over the span of the strangulation into a single cello holding a single note.

Josef's legs jerk and twitch.

Elena watches, fascinated.

The rain outside intensifies.

As the strangulation continues, a deep rumble is felt: the Furies are rising from the earth.

A dark stain appears around Josef's crotch.

When the cello's single note ends, Josef is dead.

Hamilton releases the belt, exhausted, and crumples onto his father.

ELENA: It's hard work, killing.

Elena turns to Lamb and nods toward Hamilton.

Lamb goes over to Hamilton.

HAMILTON: No, let me –

LAMB: Shh, it's over. It's over. You did good.

Lamb gently drags Hamilton away from the body.

Elena packs away all her items.

Lamb returns to Josef's body and checks for a pulse.

HAMILTON: I even know what you said to him.

ELENA: Do you?

HAMILTON: You're going to kill me anyway.

Lamb rises to his feet, his back to the audience.

ELENA: Oh, Marko. You lack imagination.

Lamb unzips his fly and urinates on Josef's body.

HAMILTON: What ... ?

ELENA: I told him Lamb's real name is Istvak Pasić. (*smiles*) Revenge would be meaningless if we allowed it to be overshadowed by a brave and noble act, don't you agree? It would lack *integrity*.

LAMB: I wouldn't bring a child into this shit-fuck world, are you crazy?

Hamilton roars in despair.

Lamb takes Elena's cellphone. He goes to the door and bangs on it twice.

LAMB: (*on phone*) Gotremni sne. Dobrezete kala naprid, otu sne za dva tenuta.

Lamb hangs up. The door unlocks from the other side. Lamb opens it and steps out into the hallway.

LAMB (O.S.): Gadjemo!

Elena shoulders her bag and looks at Josef. She is mesmerized.

Lamb returns.

LAMB: Gadjemo.

Elena hands her backpack to Lamb.

ELENA: Saga ću.

Lamb puts his hand on Elena's arm and squeezes it.

Lamb turns to head for the exit, stops. He goes to Hamilton.

LAMB: For the record, I know the difference between Latin and Greek, *kurvetino.*

He exits through the open door. Elena leans against the desk.

ELENA: We rented this building three months ago and had it transformed into a police station. Told them we were shooting a movie in here. I'd say they did a good job, wouldn't you?

(*looks at Josef's corpse*) He was the last one, you know. We've hunted them all down. The Black Wolf was killed in Tallinn two months ago. He watched in a mirror as we made his wife cut his throat.

When I was in your father's camp, I played a game with myself. I closed my eyes and imagined I was standing at my grave. And the game was to find the best inscription for the tombstone. My favourite one was 'Here lies one who has paid for the indifference of the gods.'

(*smiles*) It amuses me, that you think we would kill you. Why would we end your suffering?

(*beat*) We want you to live, to bear witness to what was done to us, to know what it feels like to live a life poisoned by hate. You'll never know a peaceful night's sleep again. You'll wake every morning no longer Marko, no longer Hamilton, but some other thing: an instrument. A monster. A gaping wound. You'll live in a world that is not simply indifferent to your suffering, but *bored* by it.

Revenge will be the only way to dignify your pain. It's in your blood now. And you'll come after me to hurt me, humiliate me, abuse me, and, even, kill / me –

HAMILTON: … and then what?

Elena stops, surprised by the question.

She opens her mouth to answer, but nothing comes out. She frowns, searches for an answer …

HAMILTON: And then what?
(*beat*)
No. (*in a whisper*) No.

Hamilton turns away from Elena.
Beat.

LAMB (O.S.): Gadjemo!

Elena doesn't move.

One of the walls reveals a figure standing behind it: THE YOUNG GIRL, *wearing a filthy purple dress.*

Elena sees Hamilton now through the gaze of the Young Girl: she sees a man suffering, in pain, a victim.

And before our eyes, without a sound or a tear or even a gesture, the fire that burns through Elena is snuffed out.

LAMB (O.S.): *(impatient)* Gadjemo!

Elena doesn't move.

Moment.

The Young Girl turns to look at Elena.

Elena turns to look at the Young Girl.

Their eyes meet and —

BLACKOUT.

ON CREATING A LANGUAGE
by Christina E. Kramer and Dragana Obradović

We are specialists in different aspects of South Slavic Studies (Kramer, linguistics; Obradović, literature). In order to create Lavinian, we began with a base translation that combined features – sound and syntax – of all of the successor languages to Serbo-Croatian: Croatian, Serbia, Bosnian and Montenegrin. While these languages have a high degree of shared features and mutual intelligibility, they all have features that suggest to speakers particular regional origin. *Butcher* is not intended to be a condemnation of any particular linguistic group; Lavinian, in our understanding, was to be a stand-in language for a war that took place in a certain geographical place at a specific time, but was not to add the political dimension of taking sides. Our language had to sound convincing, but should not belong to a specific linguistic community.

With the base translation completed, we then tried to create Lavinian through regular substitution of sounds: *a* for *o*, *e* for *i*, *l* for *r*, *b* for *p*, etc. This created a Lavinian that was a plausible-sounding language, but it was no longer a Slavic language. While speakers of Czech may not be able to follow an entire conversation in Macedonian, speakers will recognize many shared lexical roots, prepositions and other echoes of their own language. Lavinian had to have that sense of linguistic recognition for any Slavic speakers who watched the play; they should feel like they are on the verge of understanding.

In our final version of Lavinian, words were modified to change consonant clusters, roots adopted the vowels from different dialects and new words were created by combining Slavic roots with different derivational endings (e.g., the word *bolnica*, for 'hospital,' became *bolnaca*). Lavinian preserves the syntax and sound system of a South Slavic language, but it has mixed features, borrowing across language and dialect groups; it has new coinages built from Slavic material, and also from combinations of English and Slavic. Since the characters speak English, this type of language contact and cross-influence seemed natural.

Our intent in developing Lavinian was to create a language that sounds believable, is convincing for setting time and place, but universalizes the trauma of war and retribution.

Both authors are professors in the Department of Slavic Languages and Literatures at the University of Toronto. DRAGANA OBRADOVIĆ *is an assistant professor of South Slavic languages and literatures.* CHRISTINA E. KRAMER *is a professor of Slavic and Balkan languages and linguistics.*

LAVINIAN PRONUNCIATION GUIDE
by Christina E. Kramer and Dragana Obradović

The Lavinian follows the script; page numbers are provided. Below it, there are three versions:

1. Text in rough transcription, vaguely like English.

2. Text in International Phonetic Alphabet.[1] This will be very helpful to those who do not have access to a recorded text, as it is more precise than Version 1. Consult a table of the IPA for help decoding. The stressed syllable is preceded by the symbol '.

3. English translation.

GENERAL NOTES FOR VERSION 1 (TRANSCRIPTION)

Lavinian has only five vowel sounds:

a = like the *a* in *father*

e = like the *e* in *bet*

i = like the *i* in pizza, or the double *ee* in *beets.*

o = like the *o* in *boat* (avoid any diphthongization ending with the rounding of lips)

u = like the *oo* in *boot*

Stressed syllables are in ALL CAPS, e.g., [la-VI-ni-yan]

Consonant combinations with *h* are pronounced:

sh = shoe; ch = cheese; zh = pleasure, azure

Consonant combinations with *y* (e.g., *ty*, *ny*) are pronounced like the soft consonants in words like *tune* and *avenue*, i.e., with that little *y* sound combined with the consonant:

ny = onion; canyon; lute; million

The combination *dzh* resembles the *g* and *j* sounds in *George*, or *judge*.

Whenever *y* occurs after a vowel, it is consonantal like in *boy*.

---

[1] The Lavinian creators wish to thank E. Wayles Browne for his advice on the IPA transcription.

Josef Džibrilovo
  1. [YO-sef Dzhi-BRI-lo-vo]
  2. ['jɔ-sɛf dʒi-'bri-lɔ-vɔ]
  3. Josef Džibrilovo

Marko
  1. [MAR-ko]
  2. ['mar-kɔ]
  3. Marko

Gnivomir Ilić
  1. [GNI-vo-mir I-lich]
  2. ['gni-vɔ-mir 'i-litɕ]
  3. Gnivomir Ilić

Juraj Plamen
  1. [YU-ray PLA-men] (NB: *ray* rhymes with *sky*)
  2. ['ju-raj 'pla-mɛn]
  3. Juraj Plamen

Kazimir Mstijov
  1. [KA-zi-mir MSTI-yov]
  2. ['ka-zi-mir 'msti-jɔv]
  3. Kazimir Mstijov

Istvak Pasić
  1. [IST-vak PA-sich]
  2. ['ist-vak 'pa-sitɕ]
  3. Istvak Pasić

Danijel
  1. DA-ni-yel
  2. ['da-ni-yɛl]
  3. Danijel

p. 14 Ne ću vi ničo rači ...

      1. [NE chu vi NI-cho RA-chi ...]

          (NB: the accented ć in Lavinian is a softer version of č)

      2. ['nɛ tɕu vi 'ni-tʃɔ 'ra-tʃi ...]

      3. I won't tell you anything ...

p. 16 Prohapsi me.

      1. [pro-HAP-si me.]

      2. [prɔ-'hap-si mɛ.]

      3. Arrest me.

p. 22 Šta laviš vodje?

      1. [Shta LA-vish Vo-dye?]

      2. ['ʃta 'la-viʃ 'vɔ-djɛ?]

      3. What are you doing here?

Da, ritsaš.

      1. [Da, RIT-sash.]

      2. ['da, 'rit-saʃ.]

      3. Yes, you do.

Mene ne me preznameš, nelda?

      1. [ME-ne ne me PRE-zna-mesh, NEL-da?]

      2. ['mɛ-nɛ nɛ mɛ 'prɛ-zna-meʃ, 'nɛl-da?]

      3. You don't recognize me, do you?

Mi sne vu Torontu!?

      1. [MI sne vu to-RON-tu!?]

      2. ['mi snɛ vu tɔ-'rɔn-tu?!]

      3. We're in Toronto!?

Kato su me nošli? Bio som abrešan ... i nad som vu Torontu ...

      1. [KA-to su me NO-shli? BI-o som A-bre-shan ... i NAD sum vu
         to-RON-tu ...]

      2. ['ka-tɔ su mɛ 'nɔ-ʃli? 'bi-ɔ sɔm 'a-brɛ-ʃan ... i nad sɔm vu tɔ-'rɔn-tu ...]

      3. How did they find me? I was so careful ... and now I'm in Toronto ...

Isuse, ne nagu dumliti ... Vu rašiju moter, ka su mi doli ... ?

    1. [I-su-se, ne NA-gu DUM-li-ti ... Vu RA-shi-yu MO-ter, KA su
       mi DO-li ... ?]

    2. ['i-su-sɛ, nɛ 'na-gu 'dum-li-ti ... Vu 'ra-ʃi-ju 'mɔ-ter, 'ka su mi 'dɔ-li ... ?]

    3. Christ, I can't think straight ... What the hell did they give me ... ?

Moe glasči me ne jervoraju ...

    1. [MO-ye GLAS-chi me ne YER-vor-a-yu ...]

    2. ['mɔ-ɛ 'glas-tʃi mɛ nɛ 'jɛr-vɔ-a-ru ...]

    3. My eyes do not deceive me ...

p. 23 Ma daj mi pomači stekuti čizle ...

    1. [ma 'DAY mi po-'MA-chi 'STEK-u-ti 'CHIZ-le ...]
       (NB: *day* rhymes with *sky*)

    2. [ma 'daj mi pɔ-'ma-tʃi 'stɛ-ku-ti 'tʃi-zle ...]

    3. At least help me take off my boots ...

p. 24 Vola.

    1. [VO-la.]

    2. ['vɔ-la.]

    3. Thank you.

p. 29 Pomači mi da odiđem vodavde.

    1. [po-MA-chi mi da od-I-djem vo-DAV-de.]

    2. [pɔ-'ma-tʃi mi da ɔd-'i-dʒɛm vɔ-'dav-dɛ.]

    3. Get me out of here.

Rači njimu da bertam vu bolnaku.

    1. [RA-chi NYI-mu da BER-tam vu BOL-na-ku.]

    2. ['ra-tʃi 'ɲi-mu da 'bɛr-tam vu 'bɔl-na-ku.]

    3. Tell him I need to go to the hospital.

p. 30 Predaj varu, mila makico. Varu?

    1. [PRE-daj VA-ru, MI-la MA-ki-tso. VA-ru?]

    2. ['prɛ-daj 'va-ru 'mi-la 'ma-ki-tso. 'va-ru?]

    3. Water, please. Water?

Pomačí mi da odiđem vodavde!

   1. [po-MA-chi mi da od-I-dyem vo-DAV-de!]

   2. [pɔ-'ma-tʃi mi da ɔ-'di-dʑem vɔ-'dav-dɛ!]

   3. Get me out of here!

Ne znomam šta se dečova, okay? Mustam biti nevodje –

   1. [ne ZNO-mam shta se DE-cho-va, okay? MU-stam BI-ti NE-vo-dje –]

   2. [nɛ 'znɔ-mam ʃta sɛ 'dɛ-tʃɔ-va, ɔ-'kɛj? 'mus-tam 'bi-ti 'nɛ-vo-djɛ –]

   3. I don't know what is going on, okay? But I have to get somewhere –

Tanko moštrije od žuta dajinog rani, tanda nezahvolno jemamo dejče.

   1. [TAN-ko MO-shtri-ye od ZHU-ta DAY-i-nog RA-ni, TAN-da
ne-za-HVOL-no YE-ma-mo DEY-che.] (NB: *day* rhymes with *sky*)

   2. ['tan-kɔ 'mɔ-ʃtri-jɛ ɔd 'ʒu-ta 'daj-i-nɔg 'ra-ni, 'tan-da nɛ-za-'xvɔl-nɔ
'jɛ-ma-mɔ 'dɛj-tʃɛ.]

   3. How sharper than a serpent's tooth it is to have a thankless child.

Ja som ti tažio jidžek, Marko.

   1. [Ja SOM ti TAZH-i-o YI-dzhek, MAR-ko]

   2. [ja sɔm ti 'ta-ʒi-ɔ 'ji-dʑek, 'mar-kɔ.]

   3. I know you do because I taught you the language, Marko.

Vravaj mi, ne razmozgijem ničo malje nago ti ... Ali ja som, Marko. Tati je.

   1. [VRA-vaj mi, ne raz-MOZ-gi-yem NI-cho MA-lye NA-go ti ...
A-li YA som, MAR-ko. TA-ti ye.]

   2. ['vra-vaj mi, nɛ raz-'mɔz-gi-jem 'ni-tʃɔ 'ma-ʎɛ 'na-gɔ ti ... 'a-li ja sɔm,
'mar-kɔ, -'ta-ti yɛ]

   3. Believe me, I don't understand it any better than you do ... But it's
me, Marko. It's Daddy.

Da.

   1. [DA.]

   2. ['da.]

   3. Yes.

p. 31 Vola.
  1. [VO-la.]
  2. ['vo-la.]
  3. Thank you.

Bolnaka, bolnaka!
  1. [BOL-na-ka, BOL-na-ka!]
  2. ['bɔl-na-ka 'bɔl-na-ka!]
  3. Hospital, hospital!

p. 33 Hodem vu bolnaku.
  1. [HO-dem vu BOL-na-ku.]
  2. ['xɔ-dɛm vu 'bɔl-na-ku.]
  3. I'm going to the hospital.

p. 38 Sužni
  1. [SUZH-ni]
  2. ['suʒ-ni]
  3. Sužni

Jaste li Lavinijanac?
  1. [YA-ste li la-vi-ni-YA-nats?]
  2. ['ja-stɛ li la-vi-ni-'ja-nats?]
  3. Are you Lavinian?

p. 39 Kato se zavite?
  1. [KA-to se ZA-vi-te?]
  2. ['ka-tɔ sɛ 'za-vi-tɛ?]
  3. What is your name?

Voše nime?
  1. [VO-she NI-me?]
  2. ['vɔ-ʃɛ 'ni-mɛ?]
  3. Your name?

Ko su bili ljumi koi su vas davili vodje?
  1. [KO su BI-li LYU-mi KO-i vas DA-vi-li VO-dje?]

2. [kɔ su 'bi-li 'ʎu-mi 'kɔ-i su vas 'da-vi-li 'vɔ-djɛ?]
3. Who were the people who brought you here?

Njima vaza.
1. [NYI-ma VA-za.]
2. ['ɲi-ma 'va-za.]
3. It doesn't matter.

Čilemo vam pomači ali berta nam voše nime.
1. [CHI-le-mo vam PO-ma-chi A-li BER-ta nam VO-she NI-me.]
2. ['tʃi-lɛ-mɔ vam 'pɔ-ma-tʃi 'a-li 'bɛr-ta nam 'vɔ-ʃɛ 'ni-mɛ.]
3. We want to help, but we need your name.

Maje nime ne vezi.
1. [MA-ye NI-me ne VE-zi.]
2. ['ma-jɛ 'ni-mɛ nɛ 've-zi.]
3. My name is of no importance.

Ne vjirujem da mi čilete pomači ni tsikand. Znomam vodole ste.
1. [Ne VYI-ru-yem da mi CHI-le-te PO-ma-chi ni TSI-kand. ZNO-mam VO-do-le ste.]
2. [nɛ 'vji-ru-yɛm da mi 'tʃi-lɛ-tɛ 'pɔ-ma-tʃi ni 'tsi-kand 'znɔ-mam 'vɔ-dɔ-lɛ stɛ.]
3. And I don't believe for a second that you want to help me. I know where you are from.

p. 40 Kaleto dago ste je vodje?
1. [KA-le-to DA-go ste ye VO-dje?]
2. ['ka-lɛ-tɔ 'da-go stɛ jɛ 'vɔ-djɛ?]
3. How long have you been in the country?

Ka je voše sojnime?
1. [KA ye VO-she SOY-ni-me?]
2. ['ka jɛ 'vɔ-ʃɛ 'soj-ni-mɛ?]
3. What is your last name?

Sužni, Desni
1. [SUZH-ni], [DES-ni]

88

2. ['suʒ-ni], ['dɛs-ni]
3. Sužni, Desni

Kurvetino!
1. [kur-VE-ti-no!]
2. [kur-'vɛ-ti-nɔ!]
3. Whore!

p. 41 Raskomajte plaknu.
1. [ras-KO-may-te PLAK-nu.] (NB: *may* rhymes with *sky*)
2. [ras-kɔ-'maj-tɛ 'plak-nu.]
3. Open your jacket.

Nalim vas.
1. [NA-lim vas.]
2. ['na-lim 'vas.]
3. Please.

p. 45 Ne vjirujem vim. Ve ste Lavinijanac.
1. [ne VYI-ru-yem vim. VE ste la-vi-ni-YA-nats.]
2. [nɛ 'vji-ru-jɛm vim. 'vɛ stɛ la-vi-ni-'ja-nats.]
3. I don't believe you. You're Lavinian.

Talči, kurvetino.
1. [TAL-chi kur-VE-ti-no.]
2. ['tal-tʃi kur-'vɛ-ti-nɔ.]
3. Shut up, whore.

p. 48 Fjurioji
1. [FYU-ri-oy-i]
2. ['fju-ri-oj-i]
3. The Furies

Da!
1. [DA!]
2. ['da!]
3. Yes!

Fjurioji su me krobeli vu Buenos Airesu. Ti kači su me lošisilovli djejnima, vendjeljama, ne sačam se.

1. [FYU-ri-oy-i su me KRO-be-li vu BUE-nos AY-re-su. ti KA-chi su me lo-shi-SI-lov-li DYEY-ni-ma, ven-DYEL-ya-ma, ne SACH-am se.]
2. ['fju-ri-oj-i su mɛ 'krɔ-bɛ-li vu 'buɛ-nɔs 'ai-rɛ-su. ti 'ka-tʃi su mɛ lɔ-ʃi-'si-lɔv-li 'djɛj-ni-ma, vɛn-'dʑɛl-ja-ma, nɛ 'sa-tʃam sɛ.]
3. The Furies kidnapped me in Buenos Aires. Those dogs tortured me for days, weeks, I don't remember.

p. 49 Ted su voni ...

1. [TED su VO-ni ...]
2. ['tɛd su 'vɔ-ni ...]
3. When they were ...

Vispitevati.

1. [vi-spi-TE-va-ti.]
2. [vi-spi-'tɛ-va-ti.]
3. Interrogate.

Ted su te voni vispitevali, što su te voni dečeli tebi?

1. [TED su te VO-ni vi-spi-TE-va-li, shto su te VO-ni DE-che-li te-bi?]
2. ['tɛd su tɛ 'vɔ-ni vi-spi-'tɛ-va-li, ʃtɔ su tɛ 'vɔ-ni 'dɛ-tʃɛ-li tɛ-bi?]
3. When they were interrogating you, what did they occur to you?

Vaj?

1. [VAY?]
2. ['vaj?]
3. What?

Šta su vas jaskali?

1. [SHTA su vas YAS-ka-li?]
2. ['ʃta su vas 'jas-ka-li?]
3. What were they asking you?

Ne znonam zar, ali jaskali su o nošim kodstanu, Juriju. Mož su čili, da ga mestu –

1. [ne ZNO-mam zar, A-li JAS-ka-li su o NO-shim KOD-sta-nu, YU-ri-yu. MOZH su CHI-li da ga MES-tu –]

2. [nɛ 'znɔ-nam zar, 'a-li 'jas-ka-li su ɔ nɔ-ʃim 'kɔd-sta-nu, 'ju-ri-ju. 'mɔʒ su 'tʃi-li da ga 'mɛs-tu —]

3. I'm not sure why, but they were asking about our neighbour, Yuri. Maybe they wanted to find him —

p. 50 Jasi li nim račao po Yuriju?

1. [YA-si li nim RACH-a-o po YU-ri-yu?]

2. ['ja-si li nim 'ra-tʃa-ɔ pɔ 'ju-ri-ju?]

3. Did you tell them about Yuri?

Ašto?

1. [A-shto?]

2. ['a-ʃtɔ?]

3. Why?

Von je jadini koj znoma moe nime!

1. [VON ye YA-di-ni koy ZNO-ma MOY-e NI-me!]

2. ['vɔn jɛ 'jad-i-ni kɔj 'znɔ-ma 'mɔj-ɛ 'ni-mɛ!]

3. He's the only one who knows my name!

Ti! Baže te!

1. [TI, BA-zhe te!]

2. [ti, 'ba-ʒɛ tɛ!]

3. You! They're looking for you!

p. 51 Oprasi mi, oprasi mi, ja som gniv ...

1. [o-PRA-si mi, o-PRA-si mi, ya som GNIV ...]

2. [ɔ-'pra-si mi, ɔ-'pra-si mi, ja sɔm 'gniv ...]

3. Forgive me, forgive me, it's my fault ...

Daži vadovde! Brči!

1. [DA-zhi VA-dov-de! BRCH-i!]

2. ['da-ʒi 'va-dɔv-dɛ! 'br-tʃi!]

3. Get out of here! Run!

Niko ne odvidje nidje.

1. [NI-ko ne OD-vi-dye NI-dye.]

2. ['ni-kɔ nɛ 'ɔd-vi-djɛ 'ni-djɛ.]

3. No one's going anywhere.

91

p. 52 Šukaj je!

    1. [SHU-kay ye!] (NB: *kay* rhymes with *sky*)

    2. [ˈʃu-kaj jɛ!]

    3. Shoot her!

p. 54 Pretsao som ti, da je vona stavno varljava kurvetina.

    1. [PRET-sa-o som ti da ye VO-na STAV-no VAR-lya-va kur-VE-ti-na.]

    2. [ˈprɛt-sa-ɔ sɔm ti da jɛ ˈvɔ-na ˈstav-nɔ ˈvar-ʎa-va kur-ˈvɛ-ti-na.]

    3. I told you she was just a dirty whore.

p. 56 Čilimo da vespamjedate svoe zarčine sonu.

    1. [CHI-li-mo da ves-pa-MYE-da-te SVOY-e ZAR-chi-ne SO-nu.]

    2. [ˈtʃi-li-mɔ da vɛs-pa-ˈmjɛ-da-tɛ ˈsvɔj-ɛ ˈzar-tʃi-nɛ ˈsɔ-nu.]

    3. We wish you to confess your crimes to your son.

Jači se kurvetino.

    1. [YA-chi se kur-VE-ti-no.]

    2. [ˈja-tʃi sɛ kur-ˈvɛ-ti-nɔ.]

    3. Go fuck yourself, whore.

p. 57 Vajvotinja

    1. [vay-VO-ti-nya]

    2. [vaj-ˈvɔ-ti-ɲa]

    3. The Duchess

Ne.

    1. [NE.]

    2. [ˈnɛ.]

    3. No.

Vinaće murčete i mani i njiga.

    1. [VI-na-che MUR-che-te i MA-ni I NYI-ga.]

    2. [ˈvi-na-tʃɛ ˈmur-tʃɛ-tɛ iˈma-ni i ˈɲi-ga.]

    3. You will kill both of us no matter what.

p. 58 Dran te bilo kurvetino!

    1. [DRAN te BI-lo kur-VE-ti-no!]

2. ['dran tɛ 'bi-lɔ kur-'vɛ-ti-nɔ!]

3. Shame on you, whore!

p. 59 Nimajte ... ga odsrediti ... .

    1. [NI-may-te ... ga od-SRE-di-ti ...] (NB: *may* rhymes with *sky*)

    2. ['ni-maj-tɛ ... ga ɔd-'srɛ-di-ti ...]

    3. Please ... do not harm him ...

Murčete me. Nekite ga vu miru.

    1. [MUR-che-te me. NE-ki-te ga vu MI-ru.]

    2. ['mur-tʃɛ-tɛ mɛ. 'nɛ-ki-tɛ ga vu 'mi-ru.]

    3. Kill me. Leave him alone.

Vajvotinja

    1. [vay-VO-ti-nya]

    2. [vaj-'vɔ-ti-ɲa]

    3. The Duchess

Ne sačam se ...

    1. [ne SACH-am se ...]

    2. [nɛ 'sa-tʃam sɛ]

    3. [I don't remember ...]

Solizgači

    1. [so-liz-GA-chi]

    2. [sɔ-liz-'ga-tʃi]

    3. Those who grovel

p. 60 Ne.

    1. [NE.]

    2. [nɛ.]

    3. No.

p. 62 Šao mi je, Marko, šao mi je –

    1. [SHA-o mi ye, MAR-ko, SHA-o mi ye –]

    2. ['ʃa-ɔ mi jɛ, 'mar-kɔ, 'ʃa-ɔ mi jɛ –]

    3. I'm so sorry, Marko, I'm so sorry –

Zmejo! Grazna zmeja vod žine!
1. [ZME-yo! GRAZ-na ZME-ya vod ZHI-ne!]
2. ['zmɛj-ɔ! 'graz-na 'zmɛj-a vɔd 'ʒi-nɛ!]
3. Serpent! Vile snake of a woman!

Ti si kurvetina, tvaja makica je bila kurvetina, i njina makica jesto je bila kurvetina –
1. [ti si kur-VE-ti-na, TVA-ya MA-ki-tsa ye BI-la kur-VE-ti-na, i NyI-na MA-ki-tsa YE-sto ye BI-la kur-VE-ti-na –]
2. [ti si kur-'vɛ-ti-na, 'tvaj-a 'ma-ki-tsa jɛ 'bi-la kur-'vɛ-ti-na, i 'ɲi-na 'ma-ki-tsa 'jɛ-stɔ jɛ 'bi-la kur-'vɛ-ti-na –]
3. You're a whore, your mother was a whore, her mother was a whore too –

p. 63 Okay! Okay! Defta. Raču vim ... Raču vim.
1. [Okay! Okay! DEF-ta. RA-chu vim ... RA-chu vim.]
2. [ɔ-'kɛj! ɔ-'kɛj! 'dɛf-ta. 'ra-tʃu vim ... 'ra-tʃu vim.]
3. Okay! Okay! Enough. I'll ... I'll tell you.

Vajvotinja
1. [vay-VO-ti-nya]
2. [vaj-'vɔ-ti-ɲa]
3. The Duchess

Čilu da mu pakložete glasči.
1. [Chi-lu da mu pa-KLO-zhe-te GLAS-chi.]
2. ['tʃi-lu da mu pa-'klɔ-ʒɛ-tɛ 'glas-tʃi.]
3. I want him blindfolded.

Marko. Ne možu vim rači ako me glida.
1. [MAR-ko. ne MO-zhu vim RA-chi A-ko me GLI-da.]
2. ['mar-kɔ. nɛ 'mɔ-ʒu vim 'ra-tʃi 'a-kɔ mɛ 'gli-da.]
3. Marko. I cannot do it if he is looking at me.

p. 64 Da, da, mnogo klarno. Ja kaću dovariti desnu.
1. [da, da, MNO-go KLAR-no. YA KA-chu do-VA-ri-ti DES-nu]

2. [da, da, 'mnɔ-gɔ 'klar-nɔ. 'ja 'ka-tɕu dɔ-'va-ri-ti 'dɛs-nu.]

3. Yes, yes, very clear. I will speak the truth.

Bila je, bila je žina vu logru, seki ju je zonao Vajvotinja, jar je stilno nasela draljinu, purpurnu draljinu.

1. [BI-la ye, BI-la ye ZHI-na vu LOG-ru. SE-ki ye ZO-na-o Vay-VO-ti-nya, yar ye STIL-no NA-se-la DRA-lyi-nu, PUR-pur-nu DRA-lyi-nu.]

2. ['bi-la jɛ 'ʒi-na vu 'lɔg-ru, 'sɛ-ki ju jɛ 'zɔ-na-ɔ vaj-'vɔ-ti-na, jar jɛ 'stil-nɔ 'na-sɛ-la 'dra-ʎi-nu, 'pur-pur-nu 'dra-ʎi-nu.]

3. There was a, a woman in the camp, every person called her the Duchess. Because she always wore a dress, a purple dress.

Bila je omašna, Zadstaneš? Ostalim zorabljicima dala je *doru*, i nema čuge kao dore. Zonao som da som marnao nju razbeniti, razbeniti je bez kabijanja.

1. [BI-la je O-mash-na, ZAD-sta-nesh? O-sta-lim, zo-ra-BLJI-tsi-ma DA-la je DO-ru, i NE-ma CHU-ge KA-o DO-re. ZO-na-o som da som MAR-na-o nyu raz-BE-ni-ti, raz-BE-ni-ti ye bez ka-BI-ya-nya.]

2. ['bi-la jɛ 'ɔ-maʃ-na, 'zad-sta-nɛʃ? 'ɔ-sta-lim, zɔ-ra-'bʎi-tsi-ma 'da-la jɛ 'dɔ-ru, i 'nɛ-ma 'tʃu-ga 'ka-ɔ 'dɔ-rɛ. 'zɔ-na-ɔ sɔm, da sɔm 'mar-na-ɔ ɲu raz-'bɛ-ni-ti, raz-'bɛ-ni-ti jɛ bɛz ka-'bi-ja-ɲa.]

3. She was dangerous, you understand? She gave the other prisoners *hope*, and nothing is a threat like hope. I knew that I had to break her, break her without killing her.

Pazovano som dvenieset mojih vojneca ka sebe i tanio som Vajvotinju. Na sebi je vnesila purpurnu draljinu ... Onstovio som pratore barta tevarena, tako da seki vu logru je moganu šuti ... Mi je vačemo za stalicu, otrinata prima dalje ...

1. [pa-ZO-va-no som DVE-ni-yest MO-yih VOY-ni-tsa ka SE-be i TA-ni-o som vay-VO-ti-nyu. Na SE-bi ye VNE-si-la PUR-pur-nu DRA-lyi-nu ... on STO-vi-o som PRA-to-re i BAR-ta te-VA-re-na, TA-ko da SE-ki vu LOG-ru ye MO-ga-nu SHU-ti ... mi ye VA-che-mo za STA-li-tsu, o-TRI-na-ta PRI-ma DA-lye ...]

2. [pa'zɔ-vɔ sɔm 'dvɛ-ni-jɛst 'mɔj-ix 'vɔj-ni-tsa ka 'sɛ-bɛ i 'ta-ni-ɔ sɔm vaj-'vɔ-ti-ɲu. na 'sɛ-bi jɛ 'vnɛ-si-la 'pur-pur-nu 'dra-ʎi-nu ... ɔn 'stɔ-vi-ɔ sɔm 'pra-tɔ-rɛ i 'bar-ta tɛ-'va-rɛ-na, 'ta-kɔ da 'sɛ-ki vu 'lɔg-ru jɛ 'mɔ-ga-nu 'ʃu-ti ... mí jɛ 'va-tʃɛ-mɔ za 'sta-li-tsu, ɔ-'tri-na-ta 'pri-ma 'da-ʎɛ ...]

3. So I invited twelve of my men to my quarters and brought the Duchess there. She was wearing the purple dress ... I left the windows and the door open, so that everyone in camp could hear her ... We tied her on my desk, facing down ...

p. 65 I ... I moi moveci, jadin po jadin je selaju. Pronekad je bilo dvaje vo jastavrime, pronekad traje.

1. [i ... i MOY-i MOY-ve-tsi, YA-din po YA-din ye SE-la-yu. PRO-ne-kad ye BI-lo DVA-ye vo ya-ste-VRI-me, PRO-ne-kad TRA-ye.]

2. [i ... i 'mɔj-i, mɔj-i 'mɔ-ve-tsi, 'ja-din pɔ 'ja-din jɛ 'sɛ-la-ju. 'prɔ-nɛ-kad jɛ 'bi-lɔ 'dva-jɛ vɔ ja-stɛ-'vri-mɛ, 'prɔ-nɛ-kad 'tra-jɛ.]

3. And ... And my men, one by one, raped her. Sometimes it was two at a time, sometimes three.

Padrinuo som se da nekaliku od njih je jazmu vu ... od obrodi. Pretsao som vojnece da usiparne, ali to je podzelo taško jer je ona otkarvela iz, odesad. S njekih nije bilo barga, ali nekima je bilo gramljivo ... Jas som ih prešalio, naordio im da zakanaše ... Upala je vu neznavest, ali karestili sne reašljave sali jer mi je bilo zatrabno da vrešti, da nas mali da otprestanamo.

1. [pa-DRI-nu-o som se da ne-KA-li-ku od nyih ye YAZ-mu vu ... od O-bro-di ... PRE-tsa-o som SVA-ye VOY-ne-tse da u-si-PAR-ne, A-li to ye pod-ZE-lo TASH-ko yer ye O-na ot-KAR-ve-la iz, od-E-sad. SNyE-kih NI-ye BI-lo BAR-ga, A-li NE-ki-ma ye BI-lo GRAM-lyi-vo ... Ya som ih pre-SHA-li-o, na-OR-di-o im da za-KA-na-she ... U-pa-la ye vu NE-zna-vest, A-li ka-RE-sti-li sne re-ASH-lya-ve SA-li yer mi ye BI-lo ZA-trab-no da VRESH-ti, da nas MA-li da ot-pre-sta-NA-mo.]

2. [pa-'dri-nu-ɔ sɔm sɛ da nɛ-'ka-li-ku ɔd ɲih jɛ 'jaz-mu vu ... ɔd 'ɔ-brɔ-di ... 'prɛt-sa-ɔ sɔm 'svaj-ɛ 'vɔj-nɛ-tsɛ da u-si-'par-nɛ, 'a-li tɔ jɛ pɔd-'zɛ-lɔ 'taʃ-kɔ jɛr jɛ 'ɔ-na ɔt-'kar-vɛ-la iz, ɔd-'ɛ-sad. 'sɲɛ-kix 'ni-jɛ 'bilɔ

'bar-ga, 'a-li 'nɛ-ki-ma jɛ 'bi-lɔ 'gram-ʎi-vɔ ... ja sɔm íx 'prɛ-ʃa-li-ɔ, na-'ɔr-di-ɔ im da za-'ka-na-ʃe ... 'u-pa-la jɛ vu 'nɛ-zna-vɛst, 'a-li ka-'rɛs-ti-li snɛ rɛ-'aʃ-ʎa-vɛ 'sa-li jɛr mi jɛ 'bi-lɔ 'za-trab-nɔ da 'vreʃ-ti, da nas 'ma-li da ɔt-prɛ-sta-'na-mɔ.]

3. I made sure a few of them took her in the ... from behind. I asked my men to take their time, but that became difficult because she started bleeding, from, from everywhere. Some didn't care, but a few got squeamish ... I forced them, ordered them to finish ... She passed out at one point, but we used smelling salts because I needed her to keep screaming, to keep begging us to stop.

I kad su otvečeli moi moveci, bio je moj tran. I preradio som da je vodvažu – vu venom tanotku bila je prevaniše odiskrepljena da se odbrači – padrinuo som se da je volukam vu glasči kad som je udabio.

1. [i kad su ot-VE-che-li MOY-i MO-ve-tsi, BI-o ye moy TRAN. I pre-RA-di-o som da ye VOD-va-zhu – vu VE-nom ta-NOT-ku BI-la ye pre-VA-ni-she od-is-KREP-lye-na da se OD-bra-chi – Pa-DRI-nu-o som se da ye vo-LU-kam vu GLAS-chi kad som ye u-DA-bi-o.]

2. [i 'kad su ɔt-'vɛ-tʃɛ-li 'mɔj-i 'mɔ-vɛ-tsi, 'bi-ɔ jɛ mɔj 'tran. i prɛ-'ra-di-ɔ sɔm da jɛ 'vɔd-va-ʒu – vu 'vɛ-nɔm ta-'nɔt-ku, 'bi-la jɛ prɛ-'va-ni-ʃɛ ɔd-is-'krɛp-ʎɛ-na da se 'ɔd-bra-tʃi – pa-'dri-nu-ɔ sɔm se da jɛ vɔ-'lu-kam vu 'glas-tʃi kad sɔm jɛ u-'da-bi-ɔ.]

3. And when my men were done, it was my turn. And I had them untie her – at this point she was too exhausted to defend herself – and I made sure I looked into her eyes as I penetrated her.

Vonda som naordio da seki odzimne šineve –

1. [VON-da som na-OR-di-o da SE-ki OD-zim-ne SHI-ne-ve –]

2. ['vɔn-da sɔm na-'ɔr-di-ɔ da 'sɛ-ki 'ɔd-zim-nɛ 'ʃi-nɛ-vɛ –]

3. I then had everyone take out their knives –

Ne.

1. [NE.]

2. ['nɛ.]

3. No.

p. 66 Vola.
    1. [VO-la.]
    2. ['vɔ-l.a]
    3. Thank you.

... i naordio som da seki izmerkeže njen žotrb. Po jadin strikar seki.
    1. [... i na-OR-di-o som da SE-ki iz-MER-ke-zhe NYEN ZHO-trb.
       Po YA-din STRI-kar SE-ki]. (NB: *trb* almost rhymes with *curb*)
    2. [... i na-'ɔr-di-ɔ sɔm da 'sɛ-ki iz-'mɛr-kɛ-ʒɛ ɲɛn 'ʒɔ-trb. pɔ 'ja-din 'stri-
       kar 'sɛ-ki.]
    3. ... and I had them mark her on her stomach. One notch each.

Prekla si da je omrtvana.
    1. [PREK-la si da ye o-MRT-va-na.]
    2. ['prɛk-la si da jɛ ɔ-'mrt-va-na.]
    3. You said she was dead.

p. 68 Viži, kurvetino? Ne kačeš ...
    1. [VI-zhi, kur-VE-ti-no? ne KA-chesh ...]
    2. ['vi-ʒi, kur-'vɛ-ti-nɔ? nɛ 'ka-tʃɛʃ ...]
    3. You see, whore? You won't have the pleasure ...

p. 71 Vu prosiciju i čikajte moj nišak, seg.
    1. [vu pro-SI-tsi-ju i CHI-kay-te moy NI-shak, SEG.]
       (NB: *kay* and *tay* rhyme with *sky*)
    2. [vu prɔ-'si-tsi-ju i 'tʃi-kaj-tɛ mɔj 'ni-ʃak, sɛg.]
    3. Get in position and wait for my mark, go.

Gotreman, seg.
    1. [GO-tre-man, SEG.]
    2. ['gɔ-trɛ-man, sɛg.]
    3. Ready, go.

p. 72 Vukapsite, seg.
    1. [vu-KAP-si-te, SEG.]
    2. [vu-'kap-si-tɛ, sɛg.]
    3. Capture, go.

Radio tašina, seg.

    1. [RA-di-o Ta-shi-na, SEG.]

    2. ['ra-di-ɔ 'ta-ʃi-na, 'sɛg.]

    3. Radio silence, go.

Gošani provideni, seg.

    1. [GO-sha-ni pro-VI-de-ni, SEG.]

    2. ['gɔ-ʃa-ni prɔ-'vi-dɛ-ni, 'sɛg.]

    3. Targets secured, go.

Puvi najdjovenu na fonče.

    1. [PU-vi nay-DZHO-ve-nu na FON-che.]

        (NB: *nay* rhymes with *sky*)

    2. ['pu-vi naj-'dʐɔ-vi-nu na 'fɔn-tʃɛ.]

    3. Put the youngest on the phone.

Defta.

    1. [DEF-ta.]

    2. ['dɛf-ta.]

    3. Enough.

p. 73 Čikaj za podatne vugrade, seg.

    1. [CHI-kay za po-DAT-ne VU-gra-de, SEG.]

    2. ['tʃi-kaj za pɔ-'dat-nɛ 'vu-gra-dɛ, 'sɛg.]

    3. Hold and wait for further instructions, go.

Zadstaneš, seg.

    1. [zad-STA-nesh, SEG.]

    2. [zad-'sta-nɛʃ, 'sɛg.]

    3. Understood, go.

Oprasimi, tače.

    1. [o-PRA-si-mi, TA-che.]

    2. [ɔ-'pra-si-mi, 'ta-tʃɛ.]

    3. Forgive me, father.

Pogradem se na tebe, sone. Jimena taleko malo mene vu tebi.

    1. [po-GRA-dem se na TE-be, SO-ne. yi-ME-na TA-le-ko MA-lo
    ME-ne vu TE-bi.]

    2. [pɔ-'gra-dɛm sɛ na 'tɛ-bɛ, 'sɔ-nɛ. ji-'mɛ-na 'ta-lɛ-kɔ 'ma-lɔ 'mɛ-nɛ vu
    'tɛ-bi.]

    3. I'm proud of you, son. There is so little of myself in you.

Talči. Bíću olordar svojih lašjednih menata.

    1. [TAL-chi. BI-chu o-LOR-dar SVOY-ih LASH-yed-nih me-NA-ta.]

    2. ['tal-tʃi. 'bi-tɕu ɔ-'lɔr-dar 'svɔj-ix 'laʃ-jɛd-nix mɛ-'na-ta.]

    3. Shut up. I will be the master of my last minutes.

Znomaš li kako ovo unaraditi?

    1. [ZNO-mash li KA-ko O-vo u-na-RA-di-ti?]

    2. ['znɔ-maʃ li 'ka-kɔ 'ɔ-vɔ u-na-'ra-di-ti?]

    3. Do you know how to do this?

Navorno da ne.

    1. [NA-vor-no da ne.]

    2. ['na-vɔr-nɔ da nɛ.]

    3. Of course not.

p. 74 Maračeš otstenuti moje lokarče lokenima. Onda zabataj ramiš onako
svoje najstrače lokarče. Dva tupa ako mačeniš. Koda povačeš, nemoj
vrepastiti. Nemoj vrepastiti. Zadstaneš?

    1. [ma-RA-chesh ot-STE-nu-ti MOY-e LO-kar-che lo-KE-ni-ma. ON-
    da za-BA-tay RA-mish o-NA-ko SVO-ye NAY-stra-che LO-kar-
    che. Dva TU-pa A-ko ma-CHE-nish. KO-da po-VA-chesh, NE-
    moy vre-PAS-ti-ti. NE-moy vre-PAS-ti-ti. zad-STA-nesh?]
    (NB: *tay* and *nay* rhyme with *sky*)

    2. [ma-'ra-tʃɛʃ ɔt-'stɛ-nu-ti 'moj-ɛ 'lɔ-kar-tʃɛ lɔ-'kɛ-ni-ma. 'ɔn-da za-'ba-
    taj 'ra-miʃ ɔ-'na-kɔ 'svɔj-ɛ 'naj-stra-tʃɛ 'lɔ-kar-tʃɛ. dva 'tu-pa 'a-kɔ ma-
    'tʃɛ-niʃ. 'kɔ-da pɔ-'va-tʃɛʃ, 'nɛ-mɔj vrɛ-'pas-ti-ti. 'nɛ-mɔj vrɛ-'pas-ti-ti
    zad-'sta-nɛʃ?]

    3. You'll need to pin my arms with your knees. Then, wrap the belt
    around your strongest hand. Twice if you can. When you pull,
    don't relent. Don't relent. Understood?

Gotreman som.
1. [GO-tre-man som.]
2. ['gɔ-trɛ-man sɔm.]
3. I'm ready.

Ne barta mi.
1. [ne BAR-ta mi.]
2. [nɛ 'bar-ta mi.]
3. I don't need it.

Nisom pretala.
1. [NI-som PRE-ta-la.]
2. ['ni-sɔm 'prɛ-ta-la.]
3. I wasn't asking.

p. 75 Šao mi je ...
1. [SHA-o mi ye ...]
2. ['ʃa-ɔ mi jɛ ...]
3. I'm sorry ...

p. 76 Gotremni sne. Dobrezete kala naprid, otu sne za dva tenuta.
1. [go-TREM-ni sne. Do-BRE-ze-te KA-la NA-prid, O-tu sne za DVA TE-nu-ta.]
2. [gɔ-'trɛm-ni sne. dɔ-'brɛ-zɛ-tɛ 'ka-la 'na-prid, 'ɔ-tu snɛ za 'dva 'tɛ-nu-ta.]
3. We're done. Bring the car out front, we'll be there in two minutes.

Gadjemo!
1. [GA-dzhe-mo!]
2. ['ga-dʑe-mɔ!]
3. Let's go!

Saga ću.
1. [SA-ga chu.]
2. ['sa-ga tɕu.]
3. I'll be right there.

PLAYWRIGHT'S ACKNOWLEDGEMENTS

I would like to thank the following people and institutions for their help and support in bringing *Butcher* to fruition.

For their financial support, I am grateful to the Canada Council for the Arts and the Toronto Arts Council.

Guy de Carteret and Matt White at Necessary Angel for approaching me about the play and hosting the first workshop.

Vicki Stroich for being the play's first dramaturg and bringing it to the attention of Alberta Theatre Projects.

ATP's amazing team, in particular Artistic Director Vanessa Porteous, Producer Dianne Goodman and Dramaturg Laurel Green.

The cast and crew of *Butcher*'s first production, all of whom contributed to making the play better. Their names are listed on p. 9.

The wonderful team at Coach House Books, in particular Alana Wilcox, Heidi Waechtler and Sarah Smith-Eivemark.

Jonathan Bartlett for his incredible cover art.

Throughout the process, different drafts were read by friends and colleagues and their feedback was invaluable. They are listed here alphabetically: Pierre Billon, Adam Bradley, Sochi Fried, Ravi Jain, Daniel Karasik, Sarah Kitz, Matthew MacKenzie, Andrew Templeton and E. Jane Thompson.

The dedication and rigour of Christina E. Kramer and Dragana Obradović in the creation of the Lavinian language was inspiring.

Finally, I want to share a special thank you to three women for their help with *Butcher*:

Louise Arbour for taking the time to read the play, discuss it with me and write such an articulate foreword to *Butcher*. Her insight into forgiveness changed the tenor of the play's ending.

My most demanding reader, as always, is my partner in life, Aislinn Rose, who read and commented on every iteration of the play.

And finally, to Weyni Mengesha, whose intelligence and sensitivity shaped the play and made it better than I ever hoped it could be.

ABOUT THE PLAYWRIGHT

Nicolas Billon's work has been produced in Toronto, Stratford, Vancouver, New York and Paris. His book of three plays *Fault Lines: Greenland – Iceland – Faroe Islands* (Coach House) won the 2013 Governor General's Literary Award for Drama. He recently adapted his first play, *The Elephant Song*, into a feature film. Nicolas grew up in Montreal and now lives in Toronto. His website is www.nicolasbillon.com.

Typeset in Century Gothic (display font) and Albertan.

Albertan was designed by the late Jim Rimmer of New Westminster, B.C., in 1982. He drew and cut the type in metal at the 16pt size in roman only; it was intended for use only at his Pie Tree Press. He drew the italic in 1985, designing it with a narrow fit and very slight incline, and created a digital version. The family was completed in 2005 when Rimmer redrew the bold weight and called it Albertan Black. The letterforms of this type family have an old-style character, with Rimmer's own calligraphic hand in evidence, especially in the italic.

Printed at the old Coach House on bpNichol Lane in Toronto, Ontario, on Zephyr Antique Laid paper, which was manufactured, acid-free, in Saint-Jérôme, Quebec, from second-growth forests. This book was printed with vegetable-based ink on a 1965 Heidelberg KORD offset litho press. Its pages were folded on a Baumfolder, gathered by hand, bound on a Sulby Auto-Minabinda and trimmed on a Polar single-knife cutter.

Edited for the press and designed by Heidi Waechtler
Cover illustration by Jonathan Bartlett, www.bartlettstudio.com
Photo of Nicolas Billon by Trish Lindström

Coach House Books
80 bpNichol Lane
Toronto ON M5S 3J4
Canada

416 979 2217
800 367 6360

mail@chbooks.com
www.chbooks.com